The Final Crossing

Learning to Die in Order to Live

SCOTT EBERLE

Lost Borders Press

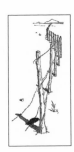

Lost Borders Press
P.O. Box 55
Big Pine, CA 93513
e-mail: meredith@lostborderspress.com
www.lostborderspress.com

© 2006, by Scott Eberle.

LOST BORDERS PRESS and colophon are registered trademarks of The
School of Lost Borders.

Library of Congress Cataloging-in-Publication Data

Eberle, Scott, 1956–

The final crossing: learning to die in order to live

cm.

ISBN 0-9777632-1-8 $19.95

1. Death and dying; 2. Ecopsychology; 3. Literary commentary

CIP

Designed by Sarah Felchlin

First Edition
Manufactured in USA

Grateful acknowledgment is made to the following for permission to reprint material that is either previously published or unpublished. Meredith Little: Excerpts from published books of Steven Foster and excerpts from her private communications with the author. Keenan Foster, Christian Foster, Selene Foster, Kevin Smith, Shelley Miller—children and stepchildren of Steven Foster: Excerpts from the unpublished journals of Steven Foster. Selene Foster, literary executor for other unpublished material by Steven Foster: Excerpts from "Under the Skirt of the Dark Goddess" and "Bring on the Maggots" by Steven Foster. Julia Gunnels, daughter of Virginia Hine: Excerpts from Last Letter to the Pebble People.

Grateful acknowledgement is also made to Museo Nacional del Prado in Madrid, Spain for permission to reproduce on the book cover a detail of the painting by Joachim Patinir: "El Paso de la Laguna Estigia"("Crossing the River Styx"). Rights reserved © Museo Nacional del Prado—Madrid.

For two people who have taught
me so much about the art of living

William Rhoads

&

Dr. John Hulcoop

and for all the men and women who,
in their final days,
taught me so much about the art of dying.

The Final Crossing

Learning to Die in Order to Live

Foreword

Early on the first morning of the year 2000, I sat facing east on an exposed ridge in Death Valley, California. Over the black silhouette of the Funeral Mountains, I watched the predawn sky catch fire, its orange and red flames licking the edge of a crescent moon. Having been alone on that ridge for four days and four nights, all I had with me were warm clothes, a sleeping bag, a simple tarp, and what remained of four gallons of water. I was nearing the end of a modern-day rite of passage, a wilderness fast commonly called a vision quest. I had come with little concern for the Y2K computer madness that some had predicted. My vigil was far more personal. I had arrived in the desert as the quintessential wounded healer, a physician so wounded that I had almost walked away from medicine. I had come to let that old physician finally die, so that someone new might be born. That new physician was due to arrive this very morning, with the rising of the sun.

The past four days in the desert had been a true revelation. Each day, I had marveled at the effects of fasting—how my body slowed to a crawl as my mind took on the wondrous awe of a child. I marveled at the daily miracle of the rising sun—how its radiant warmth is the source of all life on earth. I marveled at the infinite sky—how vast is the universe and how miniscule my role in it. I marveled at the arc of slowly moving celestial bodies—how time forever marches on ever so slowly. I marveled at the phenomenon of my singular life—how the inevitability of death makes each and every moment I have both precarious and precious. And I marveled at how, during four days of solitude, I felt more connected to other people than I had ever felt in my life.

Sitting on that ridge, I could see no other human beings. Even so, I was deeply connected with eleven others who were also fasting, each hidden from view by the undulating landscape. I was connected with three guides who maintained a central hearth at our base-camp. I was connected with a host of people whom I had wounded or who had wounded me, a connection made all the deeper by prayers for forgiveness that had filled much of my time. I was connected with long-forgotten ancestors who for thousands of years had practiced their own rites of passage in the wilderness. And I was connected with two people I had never met who had pioneered the modern form of this practice, Steven Foster and Meredith Little.

Long before my fast, Steven and Meredith had recognized the universal need of adolescents for initiation into adulthood. Drawing from a wide array of cultural sources, this husband-and-wife team began to experiment with different practices that might offer a meaningful, culturally appropriate ritual to young people. They settled on a simple yet powerful form. Each person carries an intention into the desert for four days while observing three taboos: no food, no artificial shelter, and no company. Along the way, each person "dies" as an adolescent and is "reborn" as an adult. Eventually, Steven and Meredith left this youth program in the hands of others, shifting their attention to training guides who could carry on this work, and to supporting adults who were marking various life transitions. Over three decades, Steven and Meredith had given the great gift of this ceremony, directly or indirectly, to thousands of people. I was just one of them.

I began my career as an AIDS physician. I started medical school in 1982 in San Francisco, ground zero for an epidemic that would devastate friends, families, and communities for years to come. I moved north to nearby Sonoma County in 1986 for my hospital-based training, just as the epidemic was arriving and filling up the hospital with emaciated young men. For people infected and affected by HIV, it was a desperate time. A cure seemed out of the question, and even a dignified death wasn't always possible. Feeling compelled to help, I learned quickly to respect the limits of medical technology and to honor the vast human potential of love and spirit. Suspended between these divergent truths, I grew up fast, both as a physician and as a person— maybe too fast. At the age of thirty-two, I became an AIDS specialist, and soon after that, I became the medical director for Hospice of Petaluma, the hospice in my hometown.

Early on, I learned that I was well suited for end-of-life work. To a person's bedside, I brought a gentle presence, a willingness to give over control whenever possible, and a genuine desire to serve. But I soon became addicted to the intensity of the work, and after a few years I was burned out. Away from the bedside, I was easily frustrated, often angry, and increasingly cynical. I was angry about the ravages of AIDS, about how dying people were ostracized, *and about the indifference of my community. Driven by this anger, I did some good work, but I also hurt some people. When it was my turn to be the victim of someone else's rage, this path of anger reached a sudden and abrupt end.*

One of my greatest flaws as a physician was that I naively thought it possible to be both doctor and friend to the same person. The inevitable crisis came in 1993 when a patient, who was also a friend, came to distrust both forms of our relationship. At our last clinic visit, after which we had agreed to have his care assumed by another doctor, he asked me to prescribe a medicine he could stockpile for potential suicide. When I refused, he became furious. Days later, he wrote a letter falsely accusing me of making sexual advances and sent it to anyone who had power over me—my two bosses at the HIV Clinic and at hospice, the local hospital, the State Medical Board, even a local newspaper. For the next year and a half, I battled to retain my medical license only to lose something equally valuable, the desire to be a physician. If there had been any other reasonable path to follow, I would have walked away from medicine.

Fortune, instead, granted me a year's reprieve when a Japanese medical foundation invited me to teach at a medical school in the Japanese Alps. Living alone for a year—without patient care responsibilities and without the entanglements of my own medical culture—allowed me to begin the slow process of healing. After returning home, I reluctantly resumed caring for patients, only to discover that I was now a completely different physician. Once a passionate young doctor who eschewed formal professional attire, I was now a reticent, middle-aged physician who wore a necktie as if it were a protective shield. I accepted the shift as a necessary one, but I also knew I wouldn't do my best work until I was again able to take some personal risks. I simply wasn't ready.

Providence handed me a second gift a few years after my return. Two friends, both fellow hospice workers, did four-day fasts in the desert a few months apart. Upon returning, they each told me a detailed account of what had happened to them. I was intrigued by the first story; captivated by the second. Could this be a way to mark the healing of these past years, I wondered, a way to propel me forward into a new way of practicing medicine? Six months in advance, I signed on to do a wilderness fast over the coming New Year.

I began my preparation in earnest, asking my friends and nearest colleagues to help me explore what it might mean for the old physician to die. My anger had long since abated, but my reluctance to take risks was the surest sign that I was still victim to those old wounds. The only way forward, it seemed, was to clear up the detritus of the past. The angry young physician needed to die, needed to be buried, but to let him rest I would need to do the hard work of forgiveness. This became the primary intention for my desert vigil.

For four days in the desert, I remembered, I wrote, I painted, I prayed, and I said out loud, repeatedly, "I forgive you," or "I'm sorry, please forgive me." On the fourth and final night of the fast—standing alone in the truth of who I was and who I had been—that angry, young physician finally died. On the following morning, as the sun was peaking over the jagged Funeral Mountains, a new doctor was born.

It was months before I could begin to articulate who this new physician was and what he was now called to do. Perhaps the most obvious signs of change came during the hospice home visits I was making. Having just "died" myself, I had a heightened sensitivity to the needs of people who were literally dying. I found myself taking more emotional risks with these people and staying with them for longer visits. Now, though, my work was guided by a more mature sense of limits and boundaries. I visited these people knowing I was only their doctor, not their friend.

As enthralled as I was by the way the millennium fast was transforming my hospice practice, I was equally fascinated by the potential for bringing end-of-life experience to wilderness work. Symbolic dying and literal dying are obviously not the same; yet they are deeply connected and I was determined to explore that connection. Near the end of 2000, I was back in Death Valley serving as a base-camp assistant for another group. The following summer, I completed a more formal training as a wilderness guide. Soon after that, I began leading outdoor groups of my own.

In January of 2003, my hospice work and wilderness work came together in a most unexpected way. I got an email from Patrick Clary, a friend and hospice physician who had done his own four-day desert fast with Steven and Meredith the month before. According to Patrick, Steven had a genetic lung disease that was rapidly progressing, and his doctor had told him he would do better if he lived closer to sea-level. Steven and Meredith were planning a move to a town near me and Steven would need a new physician. What was unclear from Patrick's message was whether Steven was relocating so he could live longer or so he could prepare to die. The answer, I would learn, was both. Steven was still reaching for more life, just as he was actively preparing for *his impending death. I would learn that, and so much more, during a series of home visits during the last four months of Steven's life. During that time, the two worlds I had been trying to bridge—hospice and wilderness rites of passage—merged into one.*

This book began as a simple account of the visits I made to Steven and Meredith. Very early in the writing, though, I realized the book should tell a much larger story. The coming together of these two worlds had started nearly three decades earlier. In the very same year, 1974, the first hospice in America opened, and Steven and Meredith began experimenting with the death-and-rebirth ritual of a wilderness fast. This was not mere coincidence. Both beginnings were part of the same modern reawakening, a rediscovery of the lost art of dying. At Steven's deathbed, these two worlds merged into one. This book, therefore, tells both the larger history of this coming together and the story of Steven's final crossing.

Only now do I understand when this book was first conceived. The earliest intimation of these two worlds merging into one had actually come to me several years before meeting Steven and Meredith. I was sitting on a ridge in Death Valley, watching the sun rise over the Funeral Mountains at the dawn of the new millennium.

Scott Eberle
Petaluma, California

Historical Note

The central themes of this book—Decision Road, Death Lodge, Purpose Circle, and the Great Ballcourt—are borrowed from an ancient teaching about how to die (and therefore how to live). This teaching originated in the ballcourt ceremonies of the ancient Mayans as a way of helping a ballplayer to prepare for a highly ritualized game that, on rare festival days, would culminate in a sacrificial death. It was later adapted to guide anyone who was approaching a more natural death: the old, the mortally wounded, or the seriously ill. This teaching about how to die eventually spread farther than the ballgame itself.

The origins of the Great Ballcourt can be traced back to around 1500 B.C., when rubber was first discovered by the Olmecs, the mother civilization of Mesoamerica. With the rubber ball, the Olmecs invented a rudimentary version of a ballgame that would grow in ceremonial significance for centuries to come. By 800 A.D., the Mayans were playing the game on a ceremonial ballcourt, usually built as part of a temple complex. Not unlike a modern-day basketball court, a ballcourt had two sloping walls facing one another with a stone ring suspended from each. Exact rules are not known, but the goal of the game was to send the heavy rubber ball through the ring. The ballcourt culture spread throughout Mesoamerica with variations of this heavily ritualized game also being played by the Aztecs, Zapotecs, and Toltecs. Over 600 of these courts have been unearthed in Mexico alone.

For the Mayans, the struggle between opposing teams signified the battle of life versus death, a symbolism that on certain feast days was made quite real. According to Joseph Campbell, the captain of the winning team would be beheaded on the Great Ballcourt by the captain of the losing team, a sacrifice that turned "the winner" into a god.[1] Though our modern imaginations find human sacrifice incomprehensible, this story suggests an intimacy with death lacking in our own worldview. "Times have changed," wrote Steven Foster, a few months before his own death. "If such a game existed today, it would be the losers who died. The attainment of immortality would be a minor factor."[2]

No ballcourts have been found in North America, and yet this ancient teaching traveled as far as the Midwestern plains. According to the Northern Cheyenne version of this teaching, consciously preparing for death involves four psychospiritual stages. The first is stepping onto Decision Road, which involves both recognizing that death is approaching and accepting this fact. People who remain in fierce denial, or those who die suddenly, will likely miss this critical first step and never reach the other three stages. But for people who do consciously acknowledge that death is coming, Decision Road will lead them next to the Death Lodge.

The Death Lodge is the place where a dying person receives final visitors. If old wounds still exist within any of these relationships, here will be a final chance to forgive and be forgiven. If the dying person and visitor have already done this in the past, or if they do it well during this last meeting, then they will be better able to express love and gratitude and say their final goodbyes.

From the Death Lodge, Decision Road leads next to the Purpose Circle, a place beyond the world of people. Here a dying person is called upon to do a life review, remembering with honesty both past successes and failures. For religious people, this summing up is typically done before a God. For agnostics or atheists, it is usually done alone.

Decision Road ends at the Great Ballcourt where each person "plays ball" with the Lords of Death. A place of transition—between the world of the living and the world of the dying—is common to many religious traditions, two examples being Christianity's purgatory and the bardos of Buddhism. A real-world version of this transition place is also seen in the hospice world, where a person on the verge of death may move back and forth between interacting with the living and internally preparing for death. In this way, the physical body can be considered "the ballcourt" where a person does a final dance with death.

The four-part allegory of the Great Ballcourt is used extensively in this book, because it offers evocative metaphors about the dying experience and it is an essential part of Steven Foster's story. These reasons, however, would not have been enough to justify having the allegory serve as a structure for the entire book. I do this because the allegory speaks to something universal: "the art of dying," an art which has been forgotten by many people during this past century. Consider this book one small contribution to a modern-day reawakening.

The Final Crossing

Learning to Die in Order to Live

To be blessed in death, one must learn to live.
To be blessed in life, one must learn to die.

— medieval prayer[1]

Prologue

Tuesday, May 6

"I'm not afraid of Death. No, it's the dying that scares me."

I'm sure those were Steven's words, I tell myself. *But when was that? The first visit? Or did it come later? Maybe the time he was having those terrible hallucinations. I'm not sure.*

The flow of thoughts in my head is constant, rushing ahead like the traffic around me on Geary Street. The only red light giving them pause is the neon flicker of Steven's words: "I'm not afraid of Death. No, it's the dying that scares me." I've been summoned again to his bedside, in a redwood forest on the eastern flank of Mt. Tamalpais. This, the fourth visit, will be the last. Steven Foster is now dying.

The streets are slick after several hours of rain. A shiny, thin film of water invites the slightest swerve, an unexpected crash, a sudden death. *Focus,* I tell myself. *Be Here Now.*

"Be Here Now" is the single great lesson of hospice work. With precious little future ahead, the dying person is left with only the present moment. No longer able "to do," he is left only "to be." And so it is for anyone called to sit at another person's deathbed. Show up and be present. Present for each moment, as it comes. Be Here Now.

Be here now and pay attention! I bark at myself. I scan my surroundings. A large white moving van up ahead is turning left. A man in a dark gray suit is about to cross the street.

Despite my self-admonition, I flash back to the phone call summons that came a half-hour ago from Meredith, Steven's wife of nearly thirty years. I was sitting in the stale air of a conference room in San Francisco's Hotel Nikko, surrounded by a hundred other physicians and nurses. With a morning of medical facts crammed into my head and a lunch of vegetarian pasta heavy in my belly, I was doing my mediocre-best to listen to yet another speaker. But then came the message from Meredith that awakened me. The vibration of my pager tickled the side of my waist, summoning me first to the phone and then to Steven's side.

Pay attention, I again scold myself. I see the sign for Polk Street, just ahead. *Okay, Van Ness is next. Now slow down.* I come to a full stop, look carefully to my left, then slowly make a right turn.

Steven not afraid of Death? That's easy enough to believe.

Judging from what Steven has written, and all he has said, Death has been his greatest teacher. The day Steven was first given both a diagnosis and a prognosis—an incurable lung disease with a few years to live—he gave his teacher a new name. "The Dark Goddess," he called her. "As of today I start to pray for time," he wrote that day. "I want the goddess to give me more time."[1]

For years, Steven and Meredith passed along the wisdom of this great teacher, taking people out into the desert, helping them to enact a dying-and-rebirthing ritual, the essence of any rite of passage. They understood that to "Be Here Now" at each new phase of life, you have "to die" to your old ways, so that you may be "reborn" into this new life, into each new present moment. Drawing upon the wisdom of indigenous cultures from around the world, they created a variety of ceremonies—the day walk, the night walk, the underworld journey, the earth lodge—each one rooted in lessons about living and dying that are found in the natural world. The most important was the vision quest.

As I approach the turn for Lombard Street, my attention returns to driving. *Where is it that I make the left turn? No, not this block, the next one.* Again, I consciously slow the car down as I prepare to make the turn.

You've got plenty of time to arrive, I reassure myself. *This isn't a Code Blue in the hospital.* I imagine myself dressed in surgical scrubs, racing down a dimly lit hall, sirens blaring overhead, headed to a room where someone is dying. *No, this is a death vigil. Plenty of time to sit, to watch, to listen. Plenty of time to Be Here Now.*

The next traffic light turns red and I come to a full stop.

No wait, I tell myself, *I'm not going to a death vigil. This is a dying vigil. Dying—what Steven has feared most.*

At our first home visit, Steven's most vivid words were reserved for this fear. "Suffocation terror," he called it. Exact, descriptive, piercing, his words seemed equally appropriate for a four-inch-thick medical textbook or the elegant prose of an Edgar Allan Poe story. "Suffocation" sounds horrible enough, but "suffocation terror" is even more frightening. Can fear get any worse than that? Sure it can, if it haunts you for years. A perpetual terror took Steven to some very dark places. *When I come to the last gasping breath,* he must have wondered, *how much worse will this be?*

I reach into my pocket and feel the smooth, rounded edge of a coin, the German pfennig that Steven gave me as a gift. Steven had received the coin from a group of German friends during his last trip to Europe for the first International Wilderness Guides Gathering. There in a small town near Freiburg, the group sang him an old song about the ferryman, Charon. "Fährmann, Fährmann, Fährmann hol über . . ." Charon was the boatman of Greek legend who ferried the dead across the River Styx over to Hades. In ancient times, the story goes, a family member would shut the eyes of the deceased while saying the person's name aloud, then wash the body properly and place a coin under the tongue as payment to Charon. If the preparations weren't in order, the coin not in place, then the dead person would be left on the shores of the River Styx for a hundred years. Steven gave me the pfennig, he explained, as payment to me, his hospice ferryman.

Lombard Street is a series of out-of-synch traffic lights, each red light another reminder to slow down and to look around. At the next stop, I look overhead and see darkened clouds that are threatening to burst open. When the light changes to green, again I am lost in thought.

What about Meredith and her own fear? I wonder. Over the phone, I heard that fear so clearly in her voice, however much she tried to disguise it. *What was it she said? He's drowning in his own secretions? No, that wasn't it. Secretions is doctor-speak, not a word she'd likely use. Was it phlegm? He's drowning in his own phlegm? Or just, he's drowning.* Whatever her words, the sound of her voice still echoes in my chest. I imagine her with face taut, neck twisted, and heart thumping.

Fear, an essential part of any rite of passage, would have to be part of this experience. This was one of their most important teachings: to simulate the experience of dying (so you can later be reborn), a person must face an ordeal that engenders real fear, a ritual that makes you feel as if you're sitting at death's door. This is why a desert rite of passage includes its three taboos: no company, no food, and no four-walled shelter.

But today isn't a simulation, I tell myself. Meredith's fear is as real as it gets. But what I heard on the phone wasn't just fear. It was terror. Maybe even the edge of panic.

During all their years together, Meredith was forever cast in the role of the levelheaded one, Steven's tether to a middle ground. She allowed him his flights of fancy and his dives into depression. But now, with panic approaching, she has lost that ground. I conjure up an image of her, a composite drawn from each of three home visits. Standing off to the side, one leg bent at a right angle and propped against the other. She's always been there in the background, willing to play a supporting role. Now, more than just wife and teaching partner, she has also become Steven's hospice caregiver. Nurse, home-health aide, and chaplain, all in one. These past months she surely has had more than a few moments of paralyzing fear, her own version of Steven's suffocation terror. Today was just the first time I was allowed to witness it. Steven is not the only one journeying to a new world. Meredith is, too. Today is her own rite of passage, the loss of her beloved and transition into widowhood. Until her own death comes, this may be her hardest transition of all.

Lombard Street makes a full bend to the right. I remain in the slow lane, both hands on the wheel. I keep some distance between me and the car ahead. Despite the threat of rain, the road here is dry and the driving not so dangerous.

An image of Steven flashes suddenly before me. Upright in bed, he's heaving his chest forward, gasping for air. The gurgling sound of his breath fills the room.

Good that I ordered the scopolamine patches, I reassure myself.

Often used for motion sickness, scopolamine can also slow down the secretion of fluid in the body. By minimizing respiratory secretions,

The**Hive**

Please take your book to a self
issue machine to issue to your
account – Thank you.

Surname: Jancy

First Name: Victoria

30/05/14

in particular, it can prevent "the death rattle" that can be upsetting for family and friends.

But a scopolamine patch won't dry up the fluid he already has, I remind myself. *Morphine is what really matters now.*

Morphine, the great reliever of pain, is also the perfect drug for easing shortness of breath. Months earlier, Steven declared it "a gift from Morpheus himself." Morpheus, the god of dreams, the god of sleep. Finally, Steven found a way to relieve his suffocation terror. Today he will need that morphine more than ever. He's arrived at the place he has feared for so long, the shores of the River Styx.

Lombard Street veers back to the left, then runs parallel to the edge of the San Francisco Bay. I look over the retaining wall to my right to get a view of the water, but all I can see is the Golden Gate Bridge in the distance. I've crossed this bridge hundreds of times, but now I see it as if for the first time. I see it—really *see it*—like never before.

It's a great torii gate, I suddenly realize.

A torii gate, the entrance to a Shinto shrine in Japan, is the same vermilion color as the Golden Gate. And today, on the other side of this crossing is hallowed ground, the home where Steven Foster lies dying.

He's preparing for a crossing of his own, I remind myself. *Life's final crossing. And I am his boatman, summoned to carry him to the other side.*

Still in the slow lane, I pass through the tollbooth and make my way onto the bridge. High above are the great towers looming just ahead, while off to the sides railings block a view to the cold water below.

What about me? What lies on the other side of this bridge, this crossing?

Fear suddenly turns my stomach, reminding me of the times early in my career when I would be summoned to play "the physician" in the midst of a crisis. But those responsibilities—the projections, the expectations—have long since become familiar, even comfortable. Until today, that is. Today a new version of that fear grips me. Today, I am being summoned to someone's deathbed to be more than just "the physician." I am being called to do more than just play a role. From the beginning, Steven insisted that all of me show up. Physician. Student. Wilderness guide. Friend. Confidant. Brother. Yes, he even called me "brother." And that, unbelievably, in just three visits over four short months. Three visits, soon to be four.

So where does this visit lead? Where am I headed after this, the last home visit? *Steven is dying. Meredith is becoming a widow. And Scott is . . .*

I ease off the accelerator just slightly as the bridge begins to slope down, heading toward the opposite shore.

Arriving. That's it! Scott is fully arriving, bringing "all of me" to the bedside to do this work. *Yes, I'm arriving.*

Part 1

Decision Road

Every person who elects to participate {in a symbolic death} has consciously placed her feet on decision road, the way that leads ultimately to the purpose circle of death. For this deliberate decision she must be honored, respected, and treated with the same circumspect attention a midwife gives an expectant mother. Not everybody deliberately chooses to sacrifice themselves in a symbolic death. The word sacrifice is not used flippantly. Symbolic death must involve a sacrifice—an ending. That giving up of oneself to an ending, severance, or parting is, indeed, an enactment of one's real and eventual death.

Most people would simply prefer not to think about decision road, or their inevitable death. Better to hide the absolute certainty of it with illusions of present safety, comfort, and convenience. Better to put the feet anywhere but on decision road. Hence, they are captured unaware by all the symbolic deaths the living of their life brings. At every transition they must sacrifice something of themselves. Giving up a part of themselves while at all costs avoiding decision road, invariably turns them into victims, problems, liabilities, imbalances in the social order. Many stuck in their passages never get out.[1]

– Steven Foster and Meredith Little, *The Roaring of the Sacred River*

Decision Road

The Natural World is Decision Road

For millennia, indigenous people everywhere have known how to die—
how to die symbolically and how to die physically. Living directly off
the land, much like other animals, they were exposed to the vagaries
of the natural world. Stepping onto Decision Road was not a chosen
act; it was simply a part of life. The natural world *is* Decision Road.
Everywhere around them they saw cycles of death and rebirth. The sun
sets each night, only to rise again in the morning. The moon wanes to
nothing, then waxes back to fullness. Fall decays to the dead of winter,
which yields to the resurrection of spring. An old woman dies in a
family's hut and, in the same bed, a baby is born.

In early cultures, rituals emerged as an expression of these lessons
about transformation. The elders understood that, like all other animals,
humans must battle for the right to procreate and to pass on genes, they
must battle for survival and, eventually, they must submit to death.
In a world full of chaos and disorder, ceremonies at strategic times of
life guided an individual's healthy development and also supported the
continued well-being of the tribe. First and foremost, these ceremonies
were instructive, passing along an image of the universe consistent with
that particular group's experience. They also served both a transcendent
function, awakening a sense of awe and gratitude for mystery and the
mystical, and an equally important limiting function, inculcating and
supporting the norms of a given moral order. And finally, within this
given cultural framework, they offered individual members of the
community a guide about how to live and how to die.[2]

In 1907, the anthropologist Arnold van Gennup coined the
term *rite of passage* to describe the tripartite sequence common to all
of life's great transitions: severance (*séparation*), threshold (*marge*), and
incorporation (*agrégation*).[3] *Severance* means dying to an old way of being,

threshold is the time between worlds, and *incorporation* is the rebirth into a new life. According to Joseph Campbell, this three-part schema is "the nuclear unit of the monomyth."[4] Though the details may vary, each cultural myth (and each individual person's lifestory) is a version of the hero's journey, and each journey is comprised of a series of great crossings. Conception and birth. Initiation into adulthood. Betrothal and marriage. Procreation and parenthood. Elderhood and death. "For groups, as well as for individuals," van Gennup wrote, "life itself means to separate and to be reunited, to change form and condition, to die and to be reborn. It is to act and to cease, to wait and rest, and then to begin acting again, but in a different way."[5]

In modern times, we imagine physical death to be a much greater challenge than life's other transitions, such as birth, initiation and marriage. Early people did not see such an extreme difference. They considered the entire natural world to be eternally alive, always changing and always being renewed; death of the physical body was just another transformation, just another rite of passage. Every culture had its concept of where people went after they died. Beginning with the first written account of an afterlife, nearly 4,000 years ago,[6] most of these early myths shared a few basic elements: a mountain barrier, a river, a boat and boatman, a bridge, gates and guardians, an important tree.[7] Regardless of the specific details of these afterlife stories, most early people believed that death was not an absolute and final end to life.

Journey of the Hero Twins

Though history books often speak of the Mayans as if they are extinct, their modern-day descendants can still be found in parts of Central America. The ceremonial life of these people, however, has changed considerably in the centuries following the arrival of European colonizers and missionaries. While the Mayan people have survived, the culture of the Great Ballcourt described herein has long since vanished.

The ancient Mayan ceremony of the Great Ballcourt is an example of an early people using story and ritual to explain the ongoing struggle between life and death. The Mayan people of old were farmers—their primary crop being corn—and much of their ritual life was focused on fertility rites, including the playing of the ceremonial ballgame. The ball came to symbolize the sun and the moon arcing across the sky and then disappearing into the underworld, while the ballcourt was seen as a transition zone—from drought to fertility, from life to death, from the middleworld to the underworld, and from humans to gods. In the modern Western world, the closest physical equivalents to the ballcourt are the church and the cemetery, though the ceremonies held in either lack the fertility rite aspect that was essential to the Mayan worldview.

A major source of our knowledge about the Mayans' view of death (and life) is the *Popol Vuh*, a "book of the dead" that likely began as songs and stories that were passed along orally, only later to be written down.[8] The book tells of the Hero Twins, Hunahpu and Xbalanque, and their journey to the Mayan underworld, Xibalba. Each day the fearless twins went to the Great Ballcourt to play a life-and-death game against the Lords of Death, Hun-Came and Vucub-Came; and each night they had to survive a series of equally threatening challenges. The first night was spent in the House of Gloom "where no light had ever shone," followed by nights in the House of Knives, the House of Cold, the House of Jaguars, the House of Fire, and the House of Bats.

A revealing moment in the twins' story comes during their first game on the Ballcourt, after they have survived a night in the House of Gloom. Wanting to kill the boys as quickly as possible, the Lords of Death insisted on using their own ball. As soon as the game began, they pulled out their sacrificial knives and moved toward the boys. "The first throw, and you want to kill us?" said one of the boys. "We thought that you wanted to play ball. Isn't that what your messenger said?"[9] When the boys threatened to leave, the Lords agreed to use the twins' ball. With the game now played more on their own terms, the boys displayed great agility and quickness, sending the ball through the Lords' ring and winning. Thus, they survived their first great test on the Great Ballcourt.

The text tells us that if the twins had continued playing with Death's ball, they would have been overly afraid of Death, "playing for the worm," rather than "letting the head of the [cougar] speak."[10]

A person with a worm's eye view of the world often tries to avoid any of the risks inherent in self-renewal and change. Afraid of dying, both physically and symbolically, such a person is unable to bring "all of me" to the different challenges that life will bring.

In contrast, the Hero Twins chose to play for the cougar, an essential expression of who they were and the lessons they embodied for their people. The natural world is Decision Road and it is filled with many threats—gloom and cold, jaguars and bats, knives and fire. However well the twins were to navigate these threats, they knew that one day they would have to die. But to every new challenge, each of them was determined to bring "all of me": fearlessness, wit and cunning, a willingness to enlist the help of animal allies, and an uncommon capacity to morph into whatever form a situation demands. They were willing to die symbolically and to be newly reborn, becoming more open to whatever life called out of them next. Even so, they knew that one day they would have to die physically—that, inevitably, the Lords of Death would win. "Playing for the cougar" is another way of saying that the twins had stepped consciously onto Decision Road, acknowledging that this road must lead to death.

The Great Forgetting

While modern culture claims to take a scientific approach to matters of life and death, we also have our rituals for coping with impermanence. Our primary strategy, developed over these past few centuries, has been to divorce ourselves more and more from all cycles of change. Incandescent lighting, central heating and air conditioning, and closed-in walls protect us from the extremes of weather—the Houses of Gloom, Cold and Fire. Large-scale farming, meat-packing, and markets disconnect us from the constant battle for life on the food chain—the Houses of Jaguars, Bats and Knives. The elderly living alone and the sick warehoused in institutions shield us from the blood and vomit of disease and the wasting and bloating of death—the final game played on the Great Ballcourt. And perhaps most devastating, passive large-screen entertainment has replaced the authentic storytelling that might help us comprehend the overwhelming changes that still surround us, both inside and out—the oral telling of the *Popol Vuh*. In search of creature comforts, many of us have forgotten that we are just that, creatures. We are creatures destined to change and destined to die.

In the arena of modern medicine, the mechanization of death has been particularly extreme. Before the twentieth century, most people died at home surrounded by family and friends. In a few short decades, however, doctors developed an awesome capacity to cure many illnesses and, because of that, the natural death was soon replaced by the mechanistic death of a modern hospital. To reach for the brass ring of perpetual life, an ill person had to ride the technological merry-go-round of a hospital, thereby forfeiting the possibility of a quiet death at home. The focus of medical treatment shifted from the patient—a human being with a life story—to solving problems. Doctors came to view disease as a mechanical breakdown, aging as unnatural, and death as the ultimate failure. They became so focused on mastering technology, they no longer took time to help patients decide whether they even wanted the treatments that were being planned. At its worst, this inability to communicate had doctors routinely lying to people about life-threatening diagnoses.[11]

This mechanistic approach to medical care reached its most extreme form in 1960 with the invention of cardiopulmonary resuscitation (CPR).[12] Within a few short years, the standard last rites of the hospital became a grisly scene. A person is found dead or dying in a hospital room. The wail of a Code Blue siren is triggered, which summons a bevy of doctors and nurses to the bedside. One medic shouts out orders, another pumps air into lifeless lungs, and several more take turns pounding on the dying person's frail chest, audibly cracking ribs. If death comes anyway, no stories about the person are told and no prayers are offered. Instead, the junior member of the team, a nervous intern, is left to speak with a family that has been barred from seeing this gruesome scene by hospital rules. In hopes of stealing victory from the bony hands of death, Western culture had created and sanctioned a death ritual that was, short of war, as barbaric as any we had seen in many years.

During this past century, Western civilized culture has veered farther from Decision Road than any other people in human history.

We live most of our lives hidden inside sanitized homes and offices, all signs of impermanence and death removed from view. When loved ones die anyway, we are often incredulous ("How did that happen?!"). When we dispose of their bodies, we do it quickly with a minimum of ritual. And when we are grieving, our friends and coworkers expect us to be done with the sorrow in a few short weeks, as if it could be scheduled on the calendar like a summer vacation.

When faced with a major life transition of our own, we are equally unprepared. Our culture of extreme denial has taught us to worship the ideal of the secure and stable life. Often choosing "to play for the worm," we frequently avoid life's big changes and shrink before life's big challenges. In the space of a single century, we have forgotten how to die physically and how to die symbolically. Inevitably, we also have forgotten how to live.

Call this past century the time of the Great Forgetting.

Another Hero's Journey

Many centuries after the Hero Twins' story was first told, another "hero" in the making—young Steven Foster—was initiated into adult life. Steven's rite of passage came at a graduation ceremony on the quiet Santa Barbara campus of Westmont College, a liberal arts school dedicated to the teachings of Christ. The year was 1960, the nadir of the Great Forgetting. Within that place and time, his coming-of-age ritual had been reduced to walking across a stage, collecting a diploma, and flipping a tassel from one side of a black cap to the other. On that day of graduation, Steven was declared to be "a man."

The world that awaited Steven was also on the verge of transformation, but one of a much greater kind. The cultural freeze of the '50s was about to give way to the explosiveness of the '60s. Like never before, large numbers of young people began to challenge openly the cultural beliefs and practices that they had inherited, be it with marches, sit-ins, and demonstrations, or with loud music, mind-altering drugs, and free sex. It was a tumultuous time to be stepping out into the world.

Steven began the decade innocently enough. After marrying

the daughter of the Westmont College dean, he got his doctorate in English literature from the University of Washington in Seattle. His idealized life with a young wife quickly fell apart, leading to a divorce. After remarrying and fathering a son, he started a new life as a professor at the University of Wyoming in Laramie. Never having truly come of age, Steven found himself surrounded by college students who were starting to explore new ways to do just that. Soon he, too, heard the same cultural siren that promised real transformation. In 1969, he accepted a faculty position at San Francisco State University, near one of the epicenters of this revolution.

Titles for courses Steven first taught at S.F. State were conventional: American Literature, European Literature, English Romantic Poetry, T.S. Eliot, and William Blake. As he experimented with mind-expanding drugs, though, his courses became more experimental: Science and Poetry, Literature and Consciousness, The Experience of Poetry, Psychology and English. Pushing the limits of his own conscious knowledge, he came to see education as more than reading books and listening to lectures. Learning is experience, experience is learning. Whenever possible, he stepped outside the confines of a chalkboard education—holding classes outdoors, refusing to give grades, and socializing with his students away from campus.

In 1971, Steven was fired by the university, ostensibly for his opposition to the Vietnam War, but more accurately for his refusal to play the role of traditional professor. After losing both his job and his professional identity, he began a dizzying spiral toward dissolution. Soon enough, he had lost most of his material possessions; more importantly, he had lost his wife, his children, and his family. In a word, Dr. Steven Foster "died."

In the three-part schema of a rite of passage, death is not followed immediately by rebirth. Before a person can be reborn, they must pass through the threshold phase: a confusing time of being lost between worlds, one identity having died and another still to be found. At first Steven spent this "no-name" period wandering aimlessly within the confines of the city, but soon he climbed into a Volkswagen bus and headed for the open spaces of Nevada and eastern California. For nearly a year, he roamed the back roads of these deserts—his own underworld between death and rebirth—eventually resurfacing back in the Bay Area. In the words of van Gennup, he returned home ready "to begin acting again, but in a different way."

The Symbolic Death Rediscovered

After returning from the desert, Steven took a job at a government agency for drug-addicted youth in Marin County, just north of San Francisco. Prophetically, the agency was called Rites of Passage, Inc. Here Steven was asked to create experiential trainings that would help young people learn about life and living, a teaching style similar to what had caused him trouble during his university days. In late 1974, he brought one of these offerings—a training on experiencing your own death—to the staff at the Marin Suicide Prevention and Crisis Intervention Hotline. Meredith, as one of the hotline volunteers, attended that training.

"When I asked if someone would be willing to play dead and to take a look at his or her own life from a coffin," writes Steven, "only one person stepped forward."[13] Meredith. "She said her father was gravely ill. Consequently, she had been thinking about what it means to die, for she was all too aware that death was everybody's portion. As the corpse in the coffin, she spoke of her former life in terms of light and shadow, but there was nothing she regretted."[14]

Within months, Steven also began volunteering at the hotline, where he was paired with Meredith on a weekly all-night shift. Tucked away in the small basement room of a church one night a week, they shared two responsibilities: answering calls from the suicidal and passing away late night hours when the phones were silent. Having first met through a shared fascination with death, they now came to know each other between phone calls from people who were contemplating death in a most immediate way.

> When the phones blinked red, we picked them up. I did my best to hold my own with young Meredith, for I never would have made it without her. I seriously lacked the ability to listen really carefully to what the other person was saying. Meredith was one of the best. I listened to her talking on the phone and I learned just how far one had to go before one could earn a stranger's

confidence, especially one who had swallowed pride and dialed the number of the very dread that loomed in his or her heart. Suicide! How carefully I had to listen![15]

At the time of their meeting, "death and dying" were fast becoming cultural buzzwords. Elisabeth Kübler-Ross's groundbreaking book, *On Death and Dying,* had come out five years earlier and was the cornerstone for a rapidly growing library of books on the subject.[16] The first modern-day hospice, St. Christopher's Hospice in London, was seven years old, and the first two hospices in the United States had just opened (one a short distance away in Marin). Interest in rites of passage and the symbolic death was also growing. Joseph Campbell's *Hero with a Thousand Faces* was exactly a quarter of a century old, but his writings were just now becoming popular.[17] So, too, were books on similar themes by Carlos Castaneda, Black Elk and others. The Great Forgetting was yielding quickly to the Great Remembering.

Steven's fascination with death didn't come from any direct encounters with literal death. When he was eight, his grandfather had been killed in a car accident; and during college, the sister of his fiancée had died the same way. In neither his journals nor published writings, however, did he ever mention either of these as influential. On the contrary, his fascination with death appears to have originated from his own death-and-rebirth experience.

> It occurred to me that American middle class culture was lacking certain basic initiation rites (rites of passage) that are common in many other cultures. And because young people did not undergo meaningful experiences whereby they were severed from the dependency and security of childhood, many of them were frozen in the adolescent state and never took their place among men and women as mature members of society. I examined my own childhood and saw how confusedly I entered the adult state, having never been given the chance to test and to know my own strength and ability, the only meaningful rituals being the obtaining of a driver's license, the loss of my virginity, and my going off to college. I began to realize that much of my gyrating behavior could be defined as my ignorant attempts to prove myself to myself and to my peers, so that I could satisfy my own requirements for adulthood.

I began reading books on the American Indians, looking specifically for descriptions of severance or puberty rituals that might be "therapeutically adapted" for use among middle class young people between the ages of 16 and 21. In Black Elk's The Seven Rites of the Oglala Sioux I found what I was looking for, the Hanblecheyapi ("Crying for a Vision") ritual, whereby the young person was taken away from home and parents and went alone (part-way with a guide) to the sacred mountain where he fasted, prayed, and waited for a vision, or a dream, or an unfolding of the future and his place within it, and he did not return until he was certain he had obtained what he sought, at which time he was accepted as an adult member of the tribe, with all privileges and responsibilities.[18]

Most early cultures have major rituals for marking the passage to adulthood, rituals that differ according to gender. For males, they often take the form of a physical ordeal in nature, like the "crying for a vision" ritual of the Ogalala Sioux, or "the walkabout" of the aborigines in Australia. A physical trial in nature is also part of the ancient lore for some of the world's major religions: Jesus Christ wandering in a desert wilderness for forty days being tempted by Satan, and the Buddha living for months in the depths of a forest searching for enlightenment.

Black Elk's account of the Hanblecheyapi is an inspiring description of how one culture offered a true rite of passage ceremony to its youth.[19] Given the account's emphasis on precise words to be spoken and specific rituals to be performed, however, it's hard to imagine how Steven might have adapted it for American middle-class youth. This huge creative leap was aided by many other written sources, but even more by Steven's willingness, yet again, to push the limits of conscious knowledge through direct experience. This time the experimentation was done in the natural world.

Steven's first rudimentary attempt at creating an initiation rite came in the spring of 1974, when he and Tom Pinkson co-led a three-day backpacking trip into Yosemite with thirteen young adults. Judging from Steven's diary, the key elements of what Steven and Meredith would later teach were prototypically present in this first undertaking.[20] The emphasis was on spending time alone in nature, though the solo time of two full days and three nights was relatively short. No central base-camp was kept, as each co-leader also did a solo retreat. Whether tents were used is unclear. And while some people fasted, others did not—most notably Steven.

Under the auspices of the drug abuse agency, Steven continued to take youth out on solo fasts for another year. After the first trip to Yosemite, he began taking people to the desert, the same landscape where he had done his own self-initiation. The following letter, written to one of the first desert groups, reveals the impact of these experiences.

So we endured, and we listened to the silence. At night we lay on the stony ground and watched the constellations slowly wheel across the winter sky. We fathomed loneliness. Our bellies ached, our fingers and toes were cold, we walked the four corners of the earth and we prayed, and the sound of our own voice in our own ears was strange and powerful. Perhaps we were crying to ourselves.

What did we learn? Here's something we learned, but each in his or her own way: How to endure loneliness, isolation and deprivation. Each of us learned a secret something, a way to endure, a hint at how we might survive the night and the cold and the hunger. Can you remember how you did it? That is the clue, the secret, a glimpse of the way. Do you remember how?

. . . And the waiting, waiting for time to pass, until we would again see and speak to each other. Perhaps that is a way of seeing life and death. And when we were together again do you remember what happened? Did being alone and starving help you to understand the meaning of love? I remember especially the eyes of those around me. How clear and starkly beautiful, like the atonal desert, were the eyes of those around me. People had a wise look to their face, a little older, firm yet relaxed. If the desert lured the animal from us and made us burrow and climb and shit and drink, it also lured love from our hearts. Only those who are lonely know what love is. I guess that includes almost everybody. Why do we love each other? Because we are lonely and because we can share/exchange/communicate with each other our own sense of loneliness.

It was so easy to give that night. Remember how we lay awake that night, talking, looking up at the stars, lying all in a heap? Friendship is a gift.[21]

Meredith offers her own memories of these early trips:

> After he returned, we would go for coffee or lunch, and in telling his stories, Steven would just cry. Together we began to see how important were these rites of passage, how these old ceremonies allowed people to symbolically die to their lives and step meaningfully into a new phase. We spoke of how many of the hotline callers hungered really for a symbolic death, yet had no understanding of this and nothing being provided to them, so they only saw a real death as possible. We said to each other that perhaps one day we would offer this to these hurting and suffering people. Always on the phones, one felt a bit helpless, not in giving immediate help, but because of the suffering—we knew it would go on.[22]

In 1975, Steven left the drug abuse agency, and both he and Meredith stopped their volunteer work at the hotline. Thus they began a series of life-changing transformations: friends to lovers, lovers to husband-wife, married couple to parents of a baby girl, parents to co-creators of a modern-day initiatory practice. For this last venture, a new small business of their own, they were bequeathed the name Rites of Passage, Inc. In service to a vision much bigger than their individual selves, Steven and Meredith would suffer poverty, ridicule, exhaustion, and disillusionment. "Playing for the cougar" demands nothing less.

The Natural Death Rediscovered

In October 1974, shortly before Meredith attended Steven's seminar and accepted his offer to climb into her own coffin, her father, Alden Hine, was diagnosed with inoperable lung cancer. During the early stages of his illness, Aldie—with the help of his second wife, Ginnie—actively searched for a cure. When friends and family asked what they could do to provide support, Aldie and Ginnie asked them to take a break each day at five o'clock, cocktail hour, and mentally offer them their prayers. They also encouraged people to give form to these prayers by sending a pebble, which would be placed about a fountain in their garden. This inspired a growing network of "pebble people," including many strangers who, moved by the call for support, sent pebbles of their own. Ginnie would later tell this story in her book, *Last Letter to the Pebble People*.[23]

The pebbles and prayers would not rid Aldie of his cancer, nor would traditional medical treatment. The pebble people, though, did offer essential love and support, first as Aldie fought the good fight for life and, later, as he learned to surrender into death. For Aldie, the surrendering was not merely a passive acceptance of death, a giving up. "You know," he said one day to Ginnie, "I've just realized that I'm going to have to make the same sorts of changes whether I live or die. Living well and dying well are the same thing! They require identical changes!"[24] From the beginning of his battle with cancer, he had stepped fully onto Decision Road, taking on every challenge that had come his way as consciously and proactively as possible. Whether he was facing these little deaths or the final death to come didn't matter. Like the Hero Twins of old, either way, *all of him* was showing up.

For Aldie, this conscious path could only result in one end, a natural death in the privacy of his own home. In late 1975, the American hospice movement was still in its infancy, and clusters of people were just beginning to experiment with the old ways of a home death. But when the tumor had spread to his spine, leaving him paralyzed from the waist down, Aldie insisted on going home. On the afternoon of Christmas Eve, he left the hospital for the last time and returned home. Meredith, and later Steven, traveled cross-country to join the vigil that ensued.

Without institutional rules, without tubes in orifices, without the risk of a Code Blue, Aldie and the people he most loved were set free to pursue what was most essential. For two more weeks, he drifted in and out of consciousness. Sometimes he was sleeping, sometimes interacting with visitors, and sometimes floating through his own private reality. While off in his own world, he would have conversations with a few special visitors: "Death," "Love," and "God," he called them. All were benevolent, he would tell others, even if sometimes he had to argue with them. In a hospital setting, this deathbed language would likely have been labeled as "delirium" and medicated as "a problem," but Aldie's time inside was just as vital as the more routine conversations he was having with family and friends. Both were preparations. The visitations helped Aldie, while his conversations with family and friends were to help them. When the time to die finally came, he was ready, as were they.

In her preface to Last Letter to the Pebble People, Ginnie writes:

> Perhaps the most astonishing thing we learned by participating in the death of Alden Hine was that he was not a 'victim' either of cancer or of death. He led us through the final stages of a process over which he had a remarkable degree of control. Death didn't just 'come.' Aldie worked at it, and the moment of death was his victory—and ours. I now know that those surrounding a dying person can create conditions that facilitate rather than hinder this mysterious task. A victorious death is probably as much the responsibility, and privilege, of those who love the dying person as it is of the person who is joining with his death."[25]

Aldie's victorious death forever changed Steven and Meredith. They were already beginning to see how any rite of passage is, at its core, a way to practice dying. More than just experimenting with symbolic dying, they now had been given the privilege of witnessing a real death—an experience that had all the blood and vomit of real dying, as well as the transformation and transcendence of a rite of passage. By answering honestly and courageously all that life asked of him, Aldie had rediscovered (and taught to others) a most ancient teaching. We might call this "the art of dying," but as Aldie had already learned, it is also "the art of living." The two are one and the same. This teaching would feed Steven and Meredith's work for years to come.

New Words for a New Vision

Soon after Aldie's death, Virginia "Ginnie" Hine joined Steven and Meredith in their efforts to bring rites of passage back into the modern world. She was drawn to this work because of its obvious connection to Aldie's death as well as her own work in anthropology. A former professor at the University of Florida, she had made a name for herself studying the phenomenon of human networks, seeing them as powerful tools for social and cultural transformation.[26] To Steven's inspired visions and Meredith's capacity for deep listening, Ginnie brought an anthropological framework that would guide their early experimentations.

By 1980, this work culminated in the publication of *The Book of the Vision Quest*.[27] In its first edition, Steven and Meredith describe an initiatory practice that was stripped clean of any one influence. Drawing from anthropology, myths, and poetry from all over the world, they had identified the universal elements common to any rite of passage and then tested them in the field through constant trial and error. Ultimately, their greatest teacher was the natural world itself and the people who brought back stories from their time upon the land.

Once the book was accepted for publication, Steven sent it to Hyemeyohsts Storm, a medicine teacher from the Northern Cheyenne tribe. They had never met, but Storm's book, *Seven Arrows*,[28] had been an early influence for Steven. Storm immediately recognized the importance of what he read and summoned Steven and Meredith to his home. Meredith has described that first encounter:

> We drove to Santa Barbara where he lived in a little trailer. The three of us were captivated by one other immediately. We hardly talked about our book, rather he began immediately teaching in his little trailer—the faint light shining through dusty windowpanes, he blind but deeply observant. For 24 hours, he poured his teaching into us. Not the Ballcourt teaching, not that time, but our first exposure to the four shields in its simplest form. We were blown away. It all fit so perfectly. And it was all so rich, right at a time when again we were questioning this mad vision we'd taken on to bring the vision quest back. He re-inspired us. One of the reasons we were and will be forever grateful to him. And that day he was a man. Fallible, loveable, human. Deep, powerful, reachable.[29]

Steven and Meredith's excitement is understandable. Instead of following a teacher or guru in their early years, they had created an initiatory practice for modern youth through extensive reading and then direct application and experience. Only later did Storm give them a map—ancient, yet still alive in the modern world—that described the very terrain they had been exploring. Thus began two years of Storm and his entourage appearing unannounced at Steven and Meredith's home, which was also the office of Rites of Passage, Inc. Business would go on as usual during the day—a chaos of ringing phones, meetings, people in and out—then each night Storm would wake up and teach.

On one such night, Steven, Meredith and Ginnie asked Storm

what he could tell them about dying. Meredith has written about that night:

> He taught us how his people, the Northern Cheyenne, prepared for death, a way passed down to him by the elders of his tribe. He taught us how the roots of this process (Decision Road, Death Lodge, Purpose Circle, the Ballcourt) were teachings from much farther south, how the teachings derived from the Mayan culture, the Great Ballcourt culture. He insisted we read the Popol Vuh. He said that much of the medicine wheel teachings of his tribe had originated in the Mayan and Aztec cultures.[30]

Finding such an evocative allegory was another major breakthrough for Steven and Meredith. Here was a culture-specific map, yet one that suggested something universal they could apply to their own lives and their own work. Consider all that had preceded this discovery. After losing his identity as a professor, Steven had become fascinated with the symbolic death; he and Meredith had spent years recreating a death-and-rebirth ritual for modern youth; and Aldie's last days had taught them how real death is both a physical reality and a profound opportunity for spiritual transformation. With Storm's map, they were better able to name what they had seen happen in two very different rites of passage: a young person participating in a coming-of-age ritual and a dying person preparing consciously for death. Symbolic dying and physical dying are not the same, and yet the psychospiritual stages of preparation for the two are similar. Both begin with a conscious choice to step onto Decision Road, which ultimately leads to death.

The natural world is Decision Road. Years before meeting Storm, Steven and Meredith had already committed themselves to learning from that world. With the Ballcourt map in hand, they now had a far better idea of where this chosen path might lead them. Whether in a ceremonial rite of passage or in their own living and dying, Decision Road leads to the Death Lodge, onto the Purpose Circle, and ends with a final game on the Great Ballcourt. Steven and Meredith's journey had just begun.

First Home Visit

January 4: In a few days we are moving down to sea level in Sonoma County, north of San Francisco. At the moment I seem to have contracted a terminal bronchitis, a pneumonia. My sputum continues to be yellow and I am coughing debilitating coughs 24 hours a day. The antidepressant cannot control or contain the anxiety connected to breathing difficulties. On Monday I will review with my doctor the most recent X-rays of my lungs. I am no more or less than any other bloke with this disease. The end appears to be near. For that I am thankful. Another name for death is mercy.

I will be 400 miles from my doctor, and more or less at the mercy of a totally strange environment that will cost us double what we spend here in Big Pine. I don't want to die in that environment. I want to die here in the "deepest valley." But Meredith thinks I will live longer at sea level. Prolonging the inevitable, for her sake, and for the sake of several of the kids and grandkids who live in the bay area. She has scheduled a three week teaching regimen in South Africa in April, and a huge training seminar in Big Pine in June. At the moment, I cannot see how I will be able to meet these obligations. Only time will tell.[1]

– Steven Foster, email written to a friend

January 8: We had to move from a home outside Santa Rosa, the elevation still too high for my breathing, to a place in rural Penngrove. We will be here for a couple weeks, then perhaps it's time to return home to Big Pine, to make my "last stand."

Today, while attempting to take a simple bath, I "freaked out," as the hippies used to say. There must be some fancy word for fear (phobia) of moving, even of lifting an arm to blow a dripping nose. Hyperventilation even when I am full of oxy.

My Bishop doctor has crossed my grimy paw with all the prescriptions, except, of course, dangerous drugs like morphine or marinol, both which I am curious about (the old hippie). Nothing I have seems to cut into my current run of phobias, particularly this fear of actually moving my body from the horizontal to the vertical, of putting on clothes, bathing, even eating. If I were to be given a choice, I would die without the anxiety/fear that must have been sleeping deep in the psyche until the deficiency expressed itself. Now I, formerly professor of literature and wilderness quest grandfather extraordinaire, meditate on every breath, and hear every rattle and gargle of his lungs for hour after hour in the darkness of a strange bedroom, his woman sleeping fitfully beside.[2]

– Steven Foster, email written to a friend

First Home Visit

Tuesday, January 28

Driving on Old Redwood Highway, I passed the turnoff for downtown Penngrove, a downtown all of two blocks long, and then made a left onto a small country lane. The road meandered through open fields, bordered by rickety fences and rows of native oak mixed with transplanted eucalyptus. The winter morning sun sent rays slanting through cool air washed clean by a late night storm. Cows slowly grazed on patches of sun-exposed grass enveloped in rising steam, while birds high atop the trees whistled their delight. The world was coming alive, awakening to the blue-sky promise of a new morning. It was a good day to be alive. I was both making another visit as a hospice physician *and* going to the home of the two teachers who had forever changed my life. Here was an opportunity to serve as never before.

I had already met Steven and Meredith in person once, but only briefly. Two years after my ridge-top fast in Death Valley, I had done a guide training at their wilderness school. The training had been led by two other teachers, Gigi Coyle and Roger Milliken, so the meeting with Steven and Meredith had only been a brief introduction. I had come to their school looking to see what the rites-of-passage world might have to teach me about my hospice practice. Now on this home visit, I was being asked to give something back for all that I had received. At the very least, I would offer them some information and advice; and if Steven was appropriate for hospice, I might even become his primary doctor.

At the end of the country lane, I arrived at a simple ranch-style house sitting on a small hillock with a view to the distance. It was a typical Sonoma County setting, pastoral but not breathtaking—a landscape that spoke the simple reassurance, "You're in the country now." I parked my car, pulled my stethoscope from the glove compartment, and made my way to the house.

Meredith greeted me at the door. A woman in her fifties, she had a thin, muscular body and a face filled with lines etched by long days in the sun and even longer nights in the dark with Steven. She wore a blue crystalline arrowhead on her left ear, the only adornment to a strikingly plain, yet handsome look. "Take me as I am," she seemed to tell the world.

"Scott, so good of you to come," Meredith said with a formality contradicted by her blue jeans and T-shirt.

She ushered me into a dark living room where Steven was sitting on a couch. Dressed in a plaid shirt and jeans, he had longish, gray hair tied neatly in a short ponytail. As my eyes acclimated to the poor light, I noticed an oxygen tube running from his nose, about his ears, down his neck, and out to a large tank near his feet. Next to the tank was a half-filled bottle of whiskey.

I recalled a picture I had seen of Steven when he was about forty. On his classically-chiseled face, a grin was peeking out from under a hawk-like nose. Today, nearly a quarter of a century later, those same angular features seemed softer, more vulnerable. *Is it the day-old beard, the shadows in the room, or the sagging of age and illness?* I couldn't tell.

Meredith offered me a chair directly opposite Steven and then took a spot off to the side. Though focused and present, she obviously preferred to stay in the background.

So here I am, I told myself, *sitting before Steven Foster. A man of substance, certainly. But in the end, just another fellow human with a tale to tell. A tale to tell? Isn't that what makes him unique?* Stories, the telling and the listening, had been this man's lifework.

"So, Steven, I've got nowhere to go for hours. Tell me your story."

I had cleared my morning, guessing that Steven wouldn't tolerate a hurried doctor who constantly interrupts with questions. I didn't like that mode either. A decade-plus of hospice work had taught me a most important lesson. Deep, open-ended listening is a powerful way to support another person's healing, but it takes time.

"My story?" He scanned my face as he considered his reply. "Alpha-one-antitrypsin deficiency is my story. Have you heard of it?"

I nodded yes. Alpha-one-antitrypsin deficiency is uncommon enough that I had never seen anyone with the malady, but an old classroom lecture still lingered: *a genetic deficiency of a single enzyme, alpha-one-antitrypsin, which leads to premature emphysema.* In medical school, I had been taught more about this rare disease than about how to care for someone at the end of life.

"After some searching on the internet, I came up with the diagnosis myself," said Steven with obvious pride. "Five, maybe six years ago, I asked my doctor to do the enzyme test. My level was only half-normal. That was the day I truly stepped onto Decision Road, the day I could see the end was near."

The next stop on that road, he explained, was the Jewish Hospital in Denver. There his diagnosis was confirmed and a full work-up found his breathing capacity to be 20% of normal.

"They told me my lungs were filled with holes. 'Air trapping,' the doctors called it. Swiss cheese lungs, if you ask me."

"So how are you doing now?"

"Well, one foot's in the grave already. And almost every night, the other one starts to swing over, too." He picked up one foot and plopped it down next to the other. "I wake up coughing and sputtering, with huge gobs of phlegm coming up. And always at the same time, three o'clock in the morning. A horrible way to wake up. Suffocation terror, I call it."

I felt my own throat tighten at the sound of those two words: suffocation terror.

"Doc, that's the darkest place I've known. And trust me, I've known some pretty dark places."

I felt the strong pull of his story. *Is it the drama of his struggle? Or is it the impact he's already had on my own life?* Either way, I was now a large rainbow trout, flapping away on the line, Steven reeling me in.

"But you gotta understand, if this all just ended tomorrow, I wouldn't mind." He locked eyes with me. "See, I'm not afraid of Death. No, it's the dying that scares me."

His words hung between us for a time, suspended in silence.

"Wasn't always true," he continued. "A ways back, Death had me shaking." He lifted both hands and made them quiver. "But once I got the alpha-one diagnosis, the Dark Goddess and me, we started learning how to dance together. She takes the lead and I follow. But where she wants to take me doesn't seem so bad anymore. Compared to that breathing terror, my death will be a relief. A relief and a release."

He stopped talking, his last words again hanging in silence—a silence punctuated by the drone of his ancient oxygen machine. The low-pitched hum of its motor was topped off by the swooshing rise and fall of pumped oxygen. *That noise is his constant companion,* I realized.

"Your breathing terror sounds awful," I said. "Has moving closer to sea-level made it any better?"

"Yeah, I suppose. I've felt a little stronger and the oxy level's been running a bit higher. That was my doctor's great promise. Go west old man, he said. Go west to sea-level and you'll have more time. More time for what, though, I'm not sure. Certainly for Meredith. For M, my kids and my grandkids." He turned to face her. "Though why she would still want this miserable old reprobate, I'm not sure."

Meredith walked over and put her hand on his shoulder, and he put his hand on top of hers.

"Cruel joke came when we landed here in Sonoma County," Steven continued. "My friend, Howard, offered me a place of his up in the hills. But the elevation was too high and it was in the middle of nowhere."

He described the prison-cell existence of the home in detail: the disorientation of the unfamiliar, the lack of simple distractions like television, and the twisty roads into town that made him car sick.

"So we've moved here to Howard's main home. At least for now. We're like a couple of desperadoes on the run. Holed up in these here flatlands, we're still searching for a decent hide-out."

"Where is home?" I said. "That seems to be the big question you're facing."

"You named it, doc. Where is home? One of the central struggles of life, isn't it?"

Should I interject my own story? I wondered. *Go ahead, it'll help open this up.*

"Finding home is a huge challenge," I said. I told him about *A Long Way Home,* the book I had just finished writing. A semi-autobiographical account of becoming an AIDS physician, it had taken me twenty years to live the story and eight years to write it.

He raised his eyebrows a notch, the writer and former English professor obviously intrigued. "So, doc, have you found your ever-elusive home?"

I paused to think. "Yes, I suppose so. I've been living here in Sonoma County for fifteen years now. It's the one place where I do feel like I truly belong."

"I understand just what you're saying. Two weeks ago, we left behind the one place on this earth where I belong, Big Pine and the Owens Valley. The only other home I'll ever find is the one that lies somewhere beyond this world. Where and what that's like, I haven't a clue, but that's where I'm headed. It's all in my latest book, which should be finished soon."

From a table in the corner of the room, Meredith brought me a mock-up of the book's cover. *Bound for the Crags of Ithaka,* read the title, *A Romance for Men Going Home.*

"The search for home is the eternal journey," I said. "The hero's journey."

"Yep, the one made famous by Joseph Campbell. The tales of those journeys have been handed down for countless years by storytellers from countless tribes." His tone had shifted. Not quite professorial, but the teacher was now speaking. "And most of that telling was done in a circle with a fire at its center. What Campbell did was to collect all those stories and find a few central themes. I honor him for that huge gift, for bringing those stories back into the modern world." He bowed forward, his arm across his waist.

"So tell me about this search for a temporary home," I said, "one here at sea-level. What does that look like?"

"Right now it's been reduced to a few basic questions. Where is a place with enough oxygen? And where is a place with a roof that we can afford?" He disappeared into his thoughts, his brow stitched tight. "And at the heart of them all, where is a place that I can die without being terrified?"

There's the terror again, I told myself. *"Suffocation terror."* Before me flashed an image of Steven living inside one of Rilke's poems, the tenth of the *Duino Elegies.*[3] Working deep inside a mine high in the mountains, Steven was looking for "a polished lump of primeval Pain or the petrified slag of Anger from an old volcano." *We'll need to explore that dark mine,* I told myself. *And Steven's suffocation terror is the likely portal. But be patient.*

For an end-of-life physician, the foundation of all care is "the difficult conversation:" breaking bad news, considering difficult treatment options, speaking about prognosis, contemplating a referral to hospice. What makes each of these so difficult is that the physician must risk diving deep into someone else's mine, a dark cavern filled with primal grief and rage. Even though medical school had never taught me about these conversations, the challenge of them was what I loved most about end-of-life work.

Be patient, I repeated. *First a little rapport, a little more trust.*

"Tell me, Steven, what has your doctor offered you to help with the breathing?"

"You're asking about drugs?" he answered with a smirk.

I nodded.

"Sure, I've got drugs. I have every inhaler you can imagine. Serevent, Flovent, Albuterol, Ipratropium. And of course, there's the oxy." He flapped the plastic tether that connected him to the incessant hum of the oxygen machine. "Always the oxy."

"I'm familiar with them all, Steven. All common treatments for chronic lung disease. But, to be honest, I don't know much about alpha-one-antitrypsin deficiency. That's territory for a pulmonologist." I described to him what I, a hospice specialist, could offer him—a focus on the relief of symptoms, such as pain, depression, or the suffocation terror. "But treating your specific disease, that would require a lung specialist."

"Thanks, but no thanks." He looked over to Meredith. "Already been down that road. Haven't we, M?"

Attentive as ever, Meredith met his gaze full on, nodding her head in agreement.

"We've seen some of the best specialists around," said Steven, "and they've done the best they could. We even chased down the illusory Holy Grail, a drug called Prolastin. Nope, no more of that."

"The last time was a few months ago," said Meredith. After the protracted silence, her words now carried extra weight. "We went to see a specialist in Beverly Hills. A man touted to be *the best* lung doctor in the country. He was obviously very smart, but he had no human understanding, no capacity to listen. All hot air and bluster, lecturing Steven about how he needed to be more active." I heard a razor edge to her voice that was new. "And then there was the lung transplant list. A huge gamble with a 20% success rate. Steven turned that down in a heartbeat."

"No way was I taking that hope away from someone younger," said Steven.

"But some good did come from that visit." Meredith looked over to Steven. "Made you mad as hell. Gave you the kick-start you needed."

"Damn right," he said, obviously drawing energy from her. "It gave me a second wind. For days after, I railed against the great gods of medicine. Or rather, the would-be-gods. It really was a kick in the pants."

"The renegade reborn?"

"Right on, doc. The great road of the lung specialist turned out to be a dead-end, so I went back to living life my own way."

I saw a fissure here worth exploring, a crack opened by the failure of the medical establishment. Here was a chance to explore his primordial pain, to begin that difficult conversation I'd been anticipating.

"Steven, you are on your own road, that's clear. Decision Road, you called it. Seems to me that road has brought you to a major fork."

In end-of-life work, clarifying people's goals of care is essential. It allows them first to determine what path they imagine taking, and then to choose which treatments are compatible with that path. For some, it even brings a more conscious focus to their day-to-day living.

I described two different routes I saw before Steven. One, doing everything to stay alive as long as possible. The other, focusing instead on bringing peace and comfort to each day, however many days he had left.

"It all comes down to this, Steven, what's your primary goal? Or to borrow from vision quest language, what's your intention?"

"Phewww," Steven replied, a long sigh through pursed lips. "Now you're asking the big one, doc. The million-dollar question. Is it time to live? Or is it time to die?"

He came to a full stop, losing himself in thought. I waited, but no answer came.

"So which way do you go?" I asked.

"Neither of them. Not the way you've described them anyway. Doc, this is how I see it. Just like everyone else, I'm on Decision Road. Life's highway that has to lead to death. But unlike most folks, I can see the end of the road. And it's damn close." He extended his hands out in front of him, palms up, letting them rise and fall as if they were a scale weighing out two choices. "The gods of medicine have some powerful magic," he said, letting the left hand drop as the right hand rose. "But I'm not interested in lengthening that road by a month or two—not just for the sake of survival." Then the right hand dipped as the left hand went up. "But I'm also not ready to fling myself into the arms of the Dark Goddess. I'll flirt with her, I'll dance with her, but I am not giving myself over to her. Not just yet."

Not often someone is so present with both dying and living, I thought. Most people try to deny they're dying, but when it becomes too obvious, they get overwhelmed. Not Steven. He had been dancing with this Dark Goddess for years. For someone else, this would be a difficult conversation. For him, it was a chance to share his daily reality.

"Right now," said Steven, "it's all about today. What have I got to live for today? I'll worry about tomorrow when tomorrow comes."

Sounds like a hospice approach, I thought, but I still wasn't sure. I needed to explore a little more, both his reasons for living and his readiness for dying.

"What you're describing, Steven, is a middle way. Sounds almost Buddhist."

"No, not really. Years ago I flirted with Buddhism, but I never could go for it completely. I just couldn't get behind that basic tenet of letting go, of surrendering into the One. The opposite, really. My way has always been about attachment. Fierce attachment. I'm so tied to love-karma, there's only one way forward for me. Call it the Way of Passion."

"Then that leads to another question . . ."

"Damn, doc, you are full of 'em." He smiled—the first sign of relaxation I'd noticed.

"Right you are, Steven. More questions, all designed to clarify *your* intention."

I thought back to the wilderness guide training I had done a few years earlier. The leaders, Gigi and Roger, had the participants wearing two hats; we were both people preparing to do a four-day fast and guides-in-training. A key part of both experiences was "the interview." As a person about to fast, I was invited to tell a version of my lifestory that would explain my intention for going out alone. Gigi and Roger then asked questions meant to deepen this intention by locating "the hero's journey" embedded in that story. Later, as a guide-in-training, I was then offered the chance to be one of the interviewers when another person told her story. When I returned home and resumed making hospice home visits, this search for the underlying spiritual story altered my way of talking to people who were dying.

"So here's the next question," I continued. "What's your passion? What's your reason for living? When we were talking earlier about the move to sea-level, you said you did it so you could have more time. Then you said, more time for what? So I give you back your own question. More time for what?"

"Love, love, love," he answered immediately. "Always has been the answer, always will be. More time to love. But lying around helplessly, an old wizened fool gasping for breath, a total dead-weight—that's not loving. For me, love has to be active. I'm supposed to be giving something to the world."

"And what might that something be?"

"Responding to my muse, be it writing or teaching. The only calamity that would be worse than my muse deserting me would be Meredith running off."

"And *you know* that's not happening," she said instantly.

"Yeah," Steven responded, looking at her, then back at me. "She's a bull-dog. She's dragged me across the mountain down to the ocean, just to get a few more breaths out of this tired, old carcass. I suppose she won't be leaving me anytime soon."

"So then what about your muse? Has she deserted you?"

"Yes and no. The ideas are still coming, but writing them down only gets harder. I've been reduced to pecking on a keyboard one finger at a time. This last book is almost finished, but was it ever a struggle. I'm not sure what comes next. I'm even less sure if I've got the energy for it."

"And teaching?"

"Meredith keeps putting another training in front of me. Another carrot to keep me slogging along."

When I looked to Meredith, she described how she was always testing him out, seeing if something might get him excited. A return trip to South Africa felt like too much, but a month-long training back in Big Pine had sparked his interest.

"Question is," I said to Steven, "will you feel strong enough to go back to that high of an altitude?"

He shrugged his shoulders.

"Well then, do you want to find more strength?"

"Sure I do. Of course I do. But I don't believe in the Holy Grail anymore, the great magic elixir that'll save me." He turned his gaze to the floor and then looked at me, a new challenge in his voice. "Unless you're Dr. Frankenstein and you've got some lightning that'll jolt this body back to life."

"Afraid not, Steven. No lightning, no magic elixir. But I do think you still have some options."

With a cupped right hand, he motioned for me to keep talking.

"You've come to sea-level to regain your strength, right?"

He nodded his head.

"Well, you already said that you feel stronger, that the level of oxygen in your blood has been running a little higher. So that's what you've got to build on. Consider this a time for rehabbing."

"That's right,' said Meredith, sitting upright. "His doctor back home had recommended we find him a place to rehab his lungs. Can you recommend one?"

I told them about a six-week program in Santa Rosa for people with chronic lung disease. It taught them how to breathe efficiently, how to rebuild strength, and how to get the most out of life. "Combine that with the lower elevation here and the higher concentration of blood oxygen, who knows, you might just revitalize yourself. You might give yourself another second wind."

Steven was fully engaged. I wasn't offering the Holy Grail, but I saw reflected in his eyes the possibility of more time. Not more time to be dying, but time to be living. Time for writing, for teaching, for loving.

Nope, I told myself, *he's probably not right for hospice.* He still wanted to fight for life. And if the lower elevation and rehab course helped, he might go on for another year or two. *But still, I've got to go into that dark mine of his.*

"Steven, you've told me why it is you want to keep on living. Love, you said. Love and something to give to your people. Now I want to explore what it is that might make you want to give up. To just end it all. If I remember right, you called it 'suffocation terror.'"

"That's right, doc." Steven's words seemed to sag, carrying the weight of all those late-night memories. "During the daytime I can usually find a reason to live. But in the middle of the night, it can become all too much. Sometimes I just want it to end."

"Do you ever consider suicide?"

"No, not anymore. I toyed with the idea a ways back, but decided it wasn't for me. No, I just hate flopping about for a breath, like a fish on dry ground. Damn it, just let me slide off into sweet oblivion."

"So if we could get the suffocation terror under control, then you'd have even more reason to live, right?"

"Damn straight. Give me some energy and take away that terror—that would make you a god. A real god of medicine."

"Again, Steven, no miracles here. Just a chance to improve a few symptoms. Tell me, what have you and your doctor tried to help the anxiety of breathlessness?"

He went down a long list of medicine. Several antidepressants, most recently Zoloft. Also several anxiety meds, first Xanax and then Klonopin. Even after all that, what worked best was whiskey.

"Sometimes quality stuff, but mostly rotgut like this." He tapped the bottle at his feet. "Honest, doc, it's the most reliable drug I've found. Loosens me up, makes it easier to live with the horrible fear of no-breath. And most important, it helps me to write."

"So how much are you drinking?"

"I got up to nearly a bottle a day. Had Meredith worried, so last week I stopped. Cold turkey. Was that ever a mess. I started getting the

D.T.s bad. Real bad. You remember that old song from the sixties?" He started vibrating his body, singing out loud, "Shakin' all over."

"Sounds awful."

"Yeah, it wasn't pretty. But these days, not much about me is pretty. So I'm back on the rotgut. For now anyway. But I got it down to a half-bottle a day."

"Here, Steven, I gotta be honest." I paused, not wanting to make him feel guilty. "Plain and simple, whiskey is a dirty drug. I'm not surprised it works for you. It's damn powerful stuff. But it's got way too many side-effects. Worst of all for you, it's filled with empty calories. If you want to rebuild your strength, you're going to need better nutrition."

"So how am I supposed to quit?"

I described the option of cutting down gradually, while using medicines to offset the withdrawal symptoms.

"Okay, maybe I can get off the stuff, but that still leaves me with those suffocating nights. What do I do about them?"

"Morphine, Steven. Clear and simple. Best drug there is for breathlessness. It's great for the pain center in the brain, but it also locks into where you experience shortness of breath. What you call 'suffocation terror.'"

"Whoa, now you're bringing in the big guns." His body visibly stiffened. "I'm not so sure about that. I remember what that stuff did to my father. Once he started on morphine, he got all dopey. He became so damn dependent on it, getting another hit was all he talked about. By the last week, he was hardly there."

"Morphine's a powerful drug, Steven. Just like alcohol. But you're not in your last week of life and morphine wouldn't be a sign that you were giving up. Just the opposite. If you use morphine carefully, at low dose, it'll make breathing easier for you and give you more desire to live."

That seemed to relax him some.

"Steven, as much charge as you've got around your father's death, maybe we should talk more about your own final exit. What that might look like and what hospice might do for you when the time comes."

He responded with a slight frown.

"Fair enough, not today. We've already covered enough ground."

Definitely not time for hospice, I told to myself. *Totally appropriate for morphine, but that and pulmonary rehab are what he needs. Not hospice. Not now anyway.*

We talked more about his fear of morphine, focusing on how to use it for his breathing terror. Once he had given clear consent, I pulled out my prescription pad and began to write.

Hold it, said a loud voice inside my head. *What am I doing?*

Both my jobs—the HIV Clinic and Hospice of Petaluma—were in contained systems that didn't support outside work. If Steven didn't have HIV and he wasn't appropriate for hospice, then I would be practicing medicine "off the grid." If I wrote him this prescription, I would have no malpractice insurance and no after-hours coverage from other physicians.

Oh come on, I challenged myself. *What's the risk of one prescription? Just give it to him and then sort this out later.*

I resumed writing, when suddenly I recalled the former patient of mine who had tried to ruin me years before. The scribble on the prescription pad was indecipherable, even to me.

Should I really be doing this?

As I tore up the script, another memory replaced the first, this one even stronger. I was sitting alone on the ridge in Death Valley. I was learning how to forgive, learning how to leave behind old wounds.

These are the very people who gave me that gift, I told myself. *If there's anything I can do to help them, I must.*

I wrote the prescription again, this time more slowly. As I gave the paper to Steven, my hand was still quivering, though not enough for him to notice.

Okay, I told myself, *if I'm going to give him an Rx, then I've got to take on the doctor role completely.*

I did a brief physical exam, focusing on his heart and lungs. At Meredith's request, I ordered some portable oxygen tanks by phone. We discussed the diarrhea that started whenever he had cut back on the alcohol, and then after reviewing his full list of medicines, I wrote him a prescription for a diarrhea medicine.

"Any other concerns?" I asked, my earlier fears having dissipated.

"Enough about me," said Steven. "Tell me about you. So what's your story?"

The uneasiness returned. The wilderness student in me was enticed by Steven's invitation, but the doctor was reticent. For a moment, the two battled over how to respond.

"Well, what do you want to know?" I finally said.

"Same question you had for me, doc. What's your great passion? What makes you want to live?"

No harm giving him a little of my story, I tried to reassure myself.

"Well, I think you already know that I've done several four-day fasts. Once a year now for the past three years. Starting about eighteen months ago, I also began leading outdoor trips for doctors, nurses, and therapists. Right now, the cutting edge of my inner world is exploring how to merge that outdoor work and my hospice work."

"That's great!" Steven exclaimed. "The vision quest has always been a way to practice your dying. Hospice and rites of passage should come together." He looked over at Meredith. "Damn, we should've had him with us at the hospice fast last month." He explained how they had taken eight hospice workers—doctors, nurses, chaplains, and volunteers—out for a ten-day program culminating in a four-day fast. "Of course, for a trip like that, we had to take them out to *Death Valley.*"

"Where else?" We both laughed. "Actually, I heard about the fast, but only weeks before the trip. Otherwise, I might've joined you."

Soon the roles were reversed and Steven was conducting the interview. As he dug for more details—about my life in hospice and my experience with fasting—I tried to keep him at bay. I sought a delicate balance, wanting to give him answers with substance, while still maintaining the detachment of a physician. Steven wanted none of that balance. But the more I told him, the more uneasy I became. The intimacy was like a powerful, fast-acting drug: intoxicating and quickly addictive, but with side-effects sure to come. It all peaked in a most unexpected way.

"You should lead the next hospice fast!" announced Steven, his face as alive as I'd seen it. "Yeah, doc, that would be great. I can't handle a full ten days in the desert anymore. But if you served as the lead, if you provided the ten-day anchor, Meredith and I could join the group for short stretches."

Steven Foster and Meredith Little want to partner with me? Now I was flying high. But soon enough, the side-effects began to overwhelm the pleasures. It started as uncertainty—*Am I up for this?*—escalated into anxiety, and then bordered on fear. Real fear. *I'm a doctor,* I scolded myself. *A doctor! Not his student, not a colleague, and certainly not a friend.*

"Let's do this," I said. "I leave soon for a five-day trip to Joshua Tree." I described the trip's plan. Seven doctors including me, two nurses, and an old college friend of mine. A day for arrival, another for severance and preparation, a sunrise-to-sunrise solo fast, and finally a day for stories. "Let me carry your offer into the desert. During the solo time, I'll hold your offer as my own personal intention."

"It's a deal, doc." Steven reached out to shake my hand and then reeled me in for an embrace. This big bear of a man had finally caught hold of his rainbow trout. Fortunately, his was a game of catch and release.

"One more thing before I go." I remained standing, looking first at Steven and then at Meredith. "This whole visit has been off the grid."

I explained to them about the lack of malpractice insurance and call-coverage. I had their full attention and, best I could tell, their sympathy.

"Years ago a patient got really angry with me, someone who was also a friend. It got so ugly that he tried to destroy me. And he nearly did."

I stopped talking for a moment, feeling a dark vortex of memory pulling me back. *Past history,* I told myself, resisting the pull.

"It was a big mess. Afterwards, I told myself I wouldn't ever take that risk again—the risk of being both doctor and friend. But here I am, doing just that. Again, off the grid. If you were to sue me, you might ruin me. Financially and emotionally. You wouldn't get much money, mind you, because I don't have much. But still, you could ruin me."

"Oh, but doc, why would we ever want to do that?" said Steven, his face absolutely serious.

I looked at him quizzically.

Steven glanced to his feet, shaking his head slowly. When he looked back up, he was wearing a smile as big as a crescent moon. "Doc, if you don't have any money, why would we ever bother to sue you?"

I responded with a smile of my own.

Part 2

Death Lodge

On this day and night you entertain {your loved ones} in your death lodge, a symbolic structure you have built on sacred ground. One by one you obtain closure and complete your life's relationships with them.

As you sit in the death lodge, you will finalize your will and give away all your earthly possessions. This is sacred ground. No one can come here who is not directly involved in your decision to dance on the Great Ballcourt. Those who you might have wronged or those who might still hold grudges against you are also welcomed and forgiveness sought. In the death lodge there is an important shift in the personal attitudes of the dancer. There is no longer any time to entertain uncertain unrealizable fantasies. With so little time left, the dancer sees that which is real.

When you are free of your earthly possessions and have obtained the permission of all those who came to the death lodge, you close the door to the lodge. Symbolically you end the physical part of your life. Now you are beyond the physical contact of those you love. They can only watch from afar.[1]

– Steven Foster, *The Great Ballcourt Vision Fast*

Death Lodge

A Lesson from the Bedside

You are a mortal animal and your time to die is coming soon. Imagine that you have consciously stepped onto Decision Road, that you see ahead your final game on the Great Ballcourt. Time now to prepare yourself, beginning with a visit to the Death Lodge, "a little house apart from the village where people go when they want to tell everyone they are ready to die."[2]

Perhaps you are fortunate enough to have a special place in which to do this preparation. It might be a live-in hospice, the modern-day equivalent to the Death Lodge of old, a place built specifically for the dying. Or perhaps your town has the present-day option of home hospice, a team of caregivers that helps you to spend these final days in your own home. Wherever you hold this important ritual, that Death Lodge room will become a sacred place. There, friends and family come to say goodbye. There, you bring closure to a lifetime of relationships.

According to an old hospice teaching, there are five phrases that help to complete a relationship: "Please forgive me." "I forgive you." "Thank you." "I love you." "Goodbye."[3] Speaking these words, in some form, is the essential work of the Death Lodge. Some of these final encounters are difficult. Perhaps this is so with a family member whom you've always found unapproachable in hard times, or with someone with whom you recently had a bad argument, or with an old friend you haven't seen for years. Whoever may come to the lodge, the old resentments you once had now seem inconsequential, even silly. *Look, I'm dying,* you say to yourself (and perhaps even aloud to them), *this is no time to get stuck in the past.* With whomever you meet, you find a way to offer and receive words of forgiveness, so that love and gratitude can flow easily between you. When it comes time for saying your final goodbyes, you release each other to your separate fates with the greatest of blessings.

Now imagine instead a horror-story version of your dying, a story far removed from a special room in your own home. You are faced with a serious illness, but one for which medicine has good options for treatment. Well aware of the dangers ahead, you ask your doctor to do everything possible to save your life. Complications arise, so the doctor admits you to the hospital and soon after she sends you to the intensive care unit. There, the only privacy is a curtain drawn shut on a three-sided cubicle—a space barely big enough for a bed and some machines that beep and flash to confirm you are still alive. Your most frequent visitors are a battalion of hospital staff, but their identities start to blur after yet another shift change. When your family and friends come to visit, each person is ushered in for a short time, but flashing machines and bustling nurses prevent the exchange of anything more than hopeful declarations about how well you're doing.

One day, you take a sudden turn for the worse. A lung specialist puts a breathing tube down your throat, making it impossible for you to speak. When your body starts to fight against the force of the respirator, he sedates you and paralyzes all your muscles. For days, your family and friends agonize over your condition. Might you still recover or has the situation become hopeless? Finally one day it is clear. You are dying. Everyone understands this—everyone except for you, lost in a coma.

A few brave family and friends collect at your bedside for one final vigil, one of them stepping forward to hold your hand. The lung specialist, whom a week ago you hadn't even met, slowly dials down the oxygen machine that is keeping you alive. As your heartbeat starts to slow, your brainwaves merely a flicker, one of your family bends over and whispers in your ear, "Goodbye, my dear. I love you. I am so proud of you, for all you've been and all you've done." Do you hear these words or are you too far gone for them to register? Either way, your Death Lodge is soon over.

A thousand other scenarios could be described, some in which dying at home is agonizing and ugly, and others in which the hospital offers a safe and comfortable container for a peaceful death. Which version will be your own? The values you hold and the choices you make will likely influence how the story unfolds. But prepare as you might, much of what happens may seem random and out of control. The uncertainty of it all poses a few important questions:

Do I want to postpone the work of the Death Lodge until I am actively dying, leaving it until the very end to complete my relationships?

Or would I rather heal lingering wounds throughout my life so I can keep these relationships current?

Balancing Justice and Compassion

When it comes time to say the five phrases that can heal a relationship—please forgive me, I forgive you, thank you, I love you, and goodbye—often the hardest are being forgiven and forgiving others. Forgiveness is difficult because it requires yet another step, one that must precede forgiveness. First we may have to say, "I am angry." A longer version might be, "What happened between us was painful and while I may be able to forgive you later, what you did will never be okay." If we turn the other cheek too quickly, we may risk a superficial forgiveness that appears to condone or minimize what was done, demeaning ourselves and increasing the chance of being victimized again. A mature anger, it seems, is the necessary partner of a mature capacity to forgive. By decrying what was wrong, we assert our own moral authority. Once that is done, and done well, perhaps then we can choose the high road to forgiveness. Compassion needs justice as its counterbalance, just as justice needs compassion.

Throughout his life, Steven struggled with his own anger. A crusader committed to transforming the world, to finding "justice for all," he was also an unpredictably volatile man with a sharp and mighty sword that cut both ways. Early in life, his behavior was especially erratic and the wounds he inflicted, including upon himself, were often deep. In his autobiography he identifies a primary source for his erratic nature:

> I love my mother. She's a sweet Christian woman. But she did a number on me. She raised me to think I would not be loved unless I grew up to be a good Christian gentleman. I did my best

to toe the line. It was not until I left home that I painfully and gradually began to cut myself loose from her influence. I guess I had to become thoroughly disreputable in order to dissolve the ties. In a way, my desperate quest could be defined as a search for every experience that would distress or disgust her. Why should there have been such an extreme reaction to a mother's love? What was I trying to prove? Why did I need to go that far?

"Shame on you," says my mother's conscience. "Shame and guilt. You hurt your mother. You hurt your wives. You hurt your children. You hurt yourself. But I forgive you. Jesus forgives you. He died for your sins. Accept him into your heart again and be cleansed of your sin." But I cannot. I must find my own way. This guilt and shame stuff doesn't do me any good. I should know. I whipped myself so black and blue with guilt that people couldn't live with me. "Here comes the guilty guy," they said, and went the other way.[4]

According to Elisabeth Kübler-Ross, anger is one of five innate emotions that children do not have to be taught, the others being love, fear, grief, and jealousy.[5] For centuries, civilized repression has distorted the expression of these natural emotions and this distortion often leads to harmful or self-destructive behavior. Teaching children to express their emotions in a healthy way can be challenging, yet so important. Learning how to express anger, for example, is important for establishing inner authority and outer assertiveness. Kübler-Ross insists that the healthy expression of anger should only take fifteen seconds, "long enough to say 'no thank you.'"[6]

When he was a child, Steven wasn't allowed the healthy cultivation of his inner authority and outer assertiveness. As an angry young man, he instead claimed them as his birthright, even if it meant walking a crooked path toward maturity. Again, it is important to locate Steven's childhood story within a historical frame. He grew up after World War II, a time when his parents and their peers had to hunker down to work. The dominant colors on their emotional palette were the blacks and grays of postwar grief and Cold War fear. Whatever strong emotions a person did feel were kept well hidden, and difficult conversations—whether in a hospital, a home or an office—were suppressed or avoided. Life was lived in the black-and-white suburbia of a "Leave It to Beaver" television show.

Then came the 1960s and frequent splashes of vivid emotions. In his autobiography, written years later, Steven recalls this tumultuous time:

Every now and then someone from those insane years of teaching at San Francisco State pops up into the present and says, "I remember you." I cringe inside. It's not that I'm afraid to remember. It's just that it's far easier to forget. So many of us in San Francisco, listening to rock music, smoking pot, dropping acid, dropping out, talking revolution. Black Power marching down the sacred halls of academia. Pretty girls thrusting flowers into the open muzzles of police guns. Bombs exploding in lavatories and trash cans. Straight people, gay people, poor people, people stoned on pot, LSD, speed, cocaine, heroin, marching and demanding their rights. Tac Squads bloodying heads. Bob Dylan wailing, "The times they are a'changin'."[7]

Indeed, the times were a'changin.' Every cause, every issue seemed to have its own version of liberation, its own self-declared movement. Women's lib, men's lib and gay lib. The civil right movement, the free speech movement, and the anti-war movement. Even in hospitals and clinics, there was the family practice movement, the patients' rights movement, and later the right-to-die movement. For many people, asserting moral authority, their own personal sense of justice, had become so paramount that the balance between justice and compassion was often thrown askew.

Impulsive maverick that he was, Steven lost his own balance between justice for self and compassion for others. Surrendering fully to a quest for self-discovery, he followed a path that was often self-indulgent and self-destructive. Along the way, he managed to lose two wives, two children, two stepchildren, and countless friends, while accumulating instead more than his share of emotional baggage. By the time he had reached his early thirties, a great challenge lay before him. Would he wait until he was on his deathbed to carry that burden into his Death Lodge? Or would he take on that difficult relationship work while he was still alive and well?

Learning to Release Anger

To the Death Lodge we bring our most important relationships. We want to offer love and compassion to the people who are most important to us, but past conflicts with some may have left us wounded (or we may have wounded others). In order to restore trust, a mature anger may be needed—a healthy "no, thank you" that declares the boundary between what's okay and what's not okay. As important as anger may be in asserting moral authority, sometimes that anger (or guilt or shame) can fester for too long, eating away at the soul. We can get stuck in an old story that reads, "I am, and will forever be, the victim (or perpetrator) of this wound." A deeper healing may be needed. Is it possible to unpack and release this old story, tucked deep in the psyche? Can room be made for a new story? And will this new story re-establish a balance between justice and compassion?

Around the time Steven left for his desert sojourn, Kübler-Ross began experimenting with a new way of helping people to unpack these old stories, a process she called "externalization." After years of traveling, she had become frustrated with lecturing at large auditoriums of faceless people.[8] She instead began working in more intimate settings, for longer periods of time, eventually settling on groups of up to a hundred people coming together at a retreat center for five days at a time. She and her support staff would help participants to complete their unfinished business, just as she had seen dying people do on their deathbeds.[9]

Long after Kübler-Ross had begun this work, I learned first-hand what externalization meant. The year I attended her workshop was 1988, midway through my residency training. Imagine one hundred people sitting cross-legged on the wooden floor of a large room, all facing a lead facilitator—a large, regal woman I will call "Marti." One person after another sits beside Marti on a bare mattress lying on the floor. Each person tells another story of pain: a battle with cancer, the death of a close friend, a divorce after decades of marriage. Marti conducts each person's saga as though it's a symphony of dynamic emotion. After an opening statement of the theme, the first full movement is often anger, with Marti handing the person a long rubber hose to pummel a stack of old phone books. When that shifts to a wailing cry, she hands over a knotted towel to be twisted and torn. To support a softer weeping, Marti provides a pillow to be held and caressed. Meanwhile, five other co-facilitators hover about the room, watching the audience for signs of agitation or tears, leading people one at a time to a mattress in a side-room where they can do their own externalization work.

For a culture based on emotional suppression, on avoiding the difficult conversation, this was groundbreaking work. Participants learned firsthand that the five stages of a terminal illness already described by Kübler-Ross—denial, anger, bargaining, depression, and acceptance—were just as important for anyone experiencing a major loss. When we lose someone or something deeply important to us, actively expressing and releasing our grief can help us move through and beyond the loss. If we don't do this grief work, and if the negative emotions stay bottled inside, we may perpetuate a lifestory that always leads with "I am a victim of that loss." According to Kübler-Ross, the younger we are when we begin doing this emotional unpacking, the more fully we can live afterward.[10] In her own words:

> Most people react to, rather than act in, life. Most people spend 90 percent of their energy and time worrying about tomorrows and live only 10 percent in the now. Once the pool of repressed negative emotions has been emptied, we can alter those percentages and live a much more full and gratifying and less draining and therefore less ill-health-producing life than before.[11]

Steven, Meredith, and Ginnie deeply admired Kübler-Ross's work. Both Steven and Ginnie exchanged letters with Kübler-Ross, and Ginnie actually became friends with her (Kübler-Ross wrote the foreword for *Last Letter to the Pebble People*). Even so, Steven, Meredith, and Ginnie never attended one of her workshops. By the time Steven first learned about them, he had already done his own externalization work. His, though, was a far more dangerous practice.

> [In the early 1970s] my appetite for the psychedelic state was obsessive and total. Faculty meetings, lecture halls, bedrooms, dining rooms, buses, movies, books, street corners, freeways, parks, national forests, wildernesses. Where I was, I was high. If I was in the midst of an argument with my wife, I was high. If I

was panting with desire in the arms of a woman, I was high. If I was playing with my children, I was high. If I was lecturing to my students in the classroom, I was high. And every trip I took I undid a stitch in my WASP upbringing.

The yanked out stitches oozed tears. Almost anything would set me off. Half the time I had no idea why I was crying. Sobs would explode from some deep magma chamber and I would weep for the world, for the animals, for the people, for myself—because it all seemed so beautifully futile, so right, so true, that all things should be born to one end. I <u>knew</u> with those tears. Since then I have always tried to know in this way.[12]

In a most unusual fashion, and with significant damage to his career, his family, and especially his children, Steven used psychoactive drugs to empty out a huge bucket of repressed emotions. He had spent the first thirty years of his life *reacting,* first out of obligation, then more and more out of opposition to obligation. His death as a university professor and the near-total dissolution of his family life was part of a long process of severance, a cutting away of old childhood ties of shame, guilt, and rage. He was opening a door to the possibility of personal inspiration and vision, of *acting* rather than *reacting.* A transformation that radical, however, is not done just once. It has to be worked at over many years. For Steven, the real work of the Death Lodge had only just begun.

A Lesson in Self-Forgiveness

Of the five steps that will complete a relationship (or make it current), the one over which we have the least control is "please forgive me." No matter how much we may take responsibility for our own actions, no matter how well we may express remorse or offer an apology, other people may still choose to withhold forgiveness. If compassion and mercy are not forthcoming, then "please forgive me" may need to be replaced by "I forgive myself." If a full reconciliation is not possible, then restoring the balance between justice and compassion will have to be done alone. This is some of the most difficult inner work there is to be done. For those who are able to do it, though, what was once a troublesome pain or guilt may be transformed into a deeper compassion for others who have been hurt in a similar way, perhaps even a desire to work for justice on their behalf.

In 1972, a year after losing his university job, Steven's life was in chaos. He had left his second wife, a child Keenan, and two stepchildren Kevin and Shelley; and soon after that, he fathered another son Christian, whom he also abandoned. In one of his journals, Steven describes this hard time:

> Without money, friends, or a muse, I went in search of the bundle the fool had left at the edge of the abyss just before he stepped off. The bundle didn't contain much: four children, two wives, 83 ex–lovers, 30 or more old journals, a banjo, a few books, a sleeping bag, an empty package of cigarette papers, the ghosts of my mother and father, and a yen to be fulfilled.[13]

Eventually Steven decided to run from this mess of a life, leaving by Volkswagen bus for the wastelands of Nevada. His decision to leave was yet another type of externalization: a mapping of his bleak inner world onto the landscape of a vast desert.

> I said goodbye to all my friends, most of whom weren't really friends, and hit the road for Nowhere, Nevada. As the Bay Area shrunk behind me, the enormity of what I was doing hit me hard. I was walking out on everybody. I was leaving it all behind. I was radically ducking my responsibility as a father, a breadwinner, a contributing member of society. From now on I was an outcast, an outlaw, a drifter, a deadbeat dad on the lam, a nobody. Cars streaked past me in the night. People with somewhere to go. But I had no idea where I was going.
>
> That night I drove from San Francisco to Wendover, cranking [cocaine] up my nose every half hour. Exhausted, strung out, and at wit's end, I pulled over just short of the Utah border and blacked out.
>
> The next morning I . . . looked east toward the vast expanses of the Great Salt Lake desert. Such vastness and such an inconsequential stupid life. Suddenly I was fearful of my ability to handle the vastness. My advanced degrees meant nothing here. I was nothing but a dude, the dudest of the dudes. Maybe it would be better to go back. A hundred yards away, cars roared past on the highway. The Doppler effect. Was I coming or going? I had given myself all the freedom of an outcast. Do I head east toward

Salt Lake City? Do I head south toward Las Vegas? Do I turn back toward San Francisco? Do I head north toward Twin Falls? There was a deep moment of panic. I got back in the bus, completely undecided, and turned onto the highway heading back the way I came. But I drove only as far as Wells. Wells—that's where my desert quest all began. It didn't end until I reached Death Valley, ten months later.[14]

Disappearing into the desert was a foolish act, the height of selfishness from a man whose life was out of control. Could Steven's immediate family, especially his children, ever forgive him for what he had already done and all that he was now failing to do? Could they separate the unforgivable deeds and omissions from the fallible human being that he was? Only they themselves can say.

But Steven's desert sojourn was also a brave act, a bold move toward self-forgiveness and self-renewal. As hard as it might have been for his family to forgive this man, then or now, he had the courage to climb deep into the underworld of his own soul and ask a question just as difficult. *Can I forgive myself?*

In his description of the hero's journey, Joseph Campbell tells of how a person must risk leaving home, venturing off into some kind of wilderness.[15] The hero travels into this unfamiliar realm encountering strangely intimate forces that are experienced as either severe tests or magical helpers. At a critical juncture in the journey, the hero must survive a supreme ordeal: in myths and stories, it might be battling a dragon, descending into an underworld, or being trapped in the belly of a beast. Out of that ordeal comes a great reward, a symbol of life energy that has been scaled to the hero's circumstances and needs. The hero then returns home to offer that boon to the world.

Steven's wilderness was the desert. The intimate forces he encountered were his own inner demons. The reward he sought was self-forgiveness. And the physical ordeal would come ten months into his wandering. In his autobiography, he recalls this life-changing experience, beginning with a night spent camping in the Dublin Hills, east of Salisbury Pass:

> As I recall, it was a restless night. A wind was whining through the canyon and the night was warm and dry. Memories of my

kids mingled with the dusty wind. Sighs and cries of women I'd loved echoed from the moonlit cliffs. Once again I found myself performing the litany that eased the pain. Going the rounds, asking forgiveness, trying to make it right, trying to find the words to tell them that I had to do what I did, that I had to be true to myself, that I had to follow my dream. But that night I could not rid myself of the question: What dream?

What was I doing out here, looking for clues to a mystery that could only be solved back there, with my children, amid the tangled skeins of unresolved relationships? I pitied myself that night, and despaired of ever settling the crises of my life. It seemed to me I'd been born with a fatal flaw—the reluctance to embrace the karmic consequences of my deeds. Was I doomed to be an avoider? Was I doomed to be blown hither and yon by the hot desert winds like an old scrap of newspaper?[16]

The following day he got back into his VW bus, arriving within miles at a decisive crossroad: either venture down into Death Valley in the general direction of the Bay Area, or go across the state-line back into the netherworld of Nevada. He chose the road pointing toward home.

By eight o'clock in the morning, I was down-shifting from Jubilee Pass, looking out across The Narrows to the Confidence Hills and the Owlshead Range, the morning sun coating the Panamints with golden putty. My spirits began to rise. Once again I was falling under the spell of Death Valley, drawn by its lost borders, inexhaustible mysteries and legends of dead-fall-triggers. Not many cars on the road. It was getting too hot. Sensible people stayed away from Death Valley June through September, but I felt confident I could take care of myself. I had plenty of water and a new tire—and probably something of a death wish.[17]

Foolishly, he decided to take a walk on this sizzling hot day, thinking a gallon of water and years of desert experience would keep him safe. He set out climbing up a ridge near Mormon Point, just south of Badwater, the lowest elevation in the United States. By midday he was in serious trouble. Too far from his car, on far too hot of a day, he decided to wait out the afternoon in the speckled shade of a creosote bush.

I'd done a stupid thing, but I wasn't in any real danger. I'd just rest here for a while and then I'd go back down.

As I recall, there wasn't a cloud in the sky. It was the hot, fathomless blue of azurite, a great blue corona around the unbearable dot of quicksilver that was the sun. I looked into that blue and I remembered my past again, as though it were somehow connected to the cruel blue of the Death Valley sky. I wasn't really afraid of the heat. It suited me just fine. I'd been jumping from the frying pan into the fire most of my life. I was certainly used to it by now. If I were to croak here underneath this little creosote bush, it would only be poetic justice. Like what they said back in 1899 when they found old Jim Dayton lying dead under the shade of a Death Valley mesquite: "You lived in the heat and died in the heat, and now you've gone to hell."

Hell? I hadn't done anything that bad. Would St. Peter turn me down at the golden gates for trying to find what was right for my life? Would the pain of my children not being with their father for months at a time tip the scales against my quest? Would the anger of their mothers at my not paying child support invalidate every hope? Guilt. What to do with guilt? The Protestants said, Lay your guilt at the feet of Jesus, who died for you that you might be free of it. The Catholics said, Confess. The Buddhists said, Guilt is just another manifestation of illusion. The Jews said, Obey the Law. What did Steven say? His answer lay buried in his behavior, which at that point in his life was rather bizarre, his head buried under a creosote bush, legs sticking out—like a stink beetle, nose in the sand, ass in the air, hoping that his farts would somehow save him from disaster.

The smell of the creosote bush invaded my senses—a smell of green resin mixed with yellow gypsum—an acerbic odor that sharpened the longing in my throat to drink water. The snaky branches quivered in the wind and tugged gently at the knot of my heart. Ah, I could give myself to the wind, to the mountain, to the emptiness of desert spaces, but I could not give myself to the terms of my life. I wept, seeing my children's faces. I pushed my nose into the decaying leaves and twigs and grains of sand lying under that pitiful bush and groveled in the odor of dry oxidating things.[18]

Words can only hint at a powerful experience, this epiphany that transformed Steven's lifestory. Even harder to name is "the why" of such an experience. Was it the rudimentary Death Lodge process that Steven had done with his children the night before, seeking their forgiveness?

Was it being on the verge of death, given one last chance to forgive himself? Or was it the cumulative effect of wandering through the desert of his soul for ten months, searching for clues to a deeply troubled life? Whatever the reasons, something had shifted in Steven. He now knew for certain that it was time to return home. His underworld journey was complete.

> I wanted to see my kids, get a job. Maybe meet the woman of my dreams, maybe not. Maybe live to become an accomplished ascetic in the yoga of desert rapture. Maybe not. In the end, what would it matter? I was so far behind Love I'd have to run twice as hard to catch up. But I was resolved to give it a try.[19]

A fallible man, but one determined to redeem himself, Steven would spend the rest of his life running twice as hard trying to catch up, especially with his children. But in the vast deserts of Nevada and eastern California, an old story had reached its end. Steven had left the Bay Area as "the guilty guy," a man walking backward into his future, forever obsessed by past mistakes. Out in the desert wilderness, he had done battle with his demons, eventually winning the great reward of self-forgiveness. But such a prize is ephemeral. It has to be rediscovered again and again. Under the dappled shade of a creosote bush in the noon-day heat of scorching Death Valley, Steven had entered a makeshift Death Lodge. For the rest of his life, he would be inspired to recreate that experience, over and over.

A Lesson in Gratitude

On any given day, the story of "who I am" can be told in many ways, with every potential storyline holding some part of a fuller truth. Depending on life circumstance, the dominant storyline that we choose can be optimistic and open, bitter and resigned, or somewhere in-between. Every one of us, in some ways, is "blessed" to be in this world; *and* every one of us is "cursed." The balance between blessings and curses will vary from person to person, and yet each of us has the potential to shift our relationship with our given circumstances. The more we are able to do the hard work of the Death Lodge, healing wounds already incurred, the freer we may be to choose a storyline that is present tense, life-affirming, and open to the future. "I forgive me," "I forgive you" and "please forgive me" offer the possibility of saying a more resounding "thank you" to life. A fuller version might be, "Thank you for the bounties I do have, *right now,* and thank you for the possibilities that the future may bring."

In spite of the self-forgiveness that Steven found in the desert, the circumstances awaiting his return home were still abysmal. He had no money, no job, no work identity, no life partner, and fractured relationships with each of his children. Saying "thank you" to his life could not have been easy. This journal entry, written less than a year after the desert sojourn, captures how he often struggled with despair:

> Woke up in the middle of the night. Couldn't get back to sleep. Listened to the sound of [my girlfriend's] steady breathing and began to project the future from here, as I sit bare-assed in her cold living room hearing the distant hum of a diesel locomotive. Earlier, yesterday morning, I had awakened to thoughts of suicide. The idea abated, became submerged in the flow of another day. But now the image of death has resurfaced and again I wrestle with the angel of darkness.
>
> I do not understand why, at this time of my life, my health should be so poor, my pocket book so empty, my love in such despair. I realize the fortunes of any man ebb and flow and that, at any rate, this life is but a shadow, a chimerical dream of reality. Nevertheless, I live as though this is the only life. How can I ever know another as infinitely sweet and infinitely sad?
>
> I feel no self-pity—only a dull and half-hearted hatred of circumstances. O my children. Your father never forgot you. Never for an instant.[20]

Despite his struggles with despair, Steven's desert lesson in self-forgiveness offered him the possibility of being grateful for what he did have. He was grateful to be alive. He was grateful for the possibility of redeeming himself. He was grateful that he might again become more of "a hero" and less of "a villain" to the people he loved.

To rewrite his lifestory, though, first Steven would have to prove himself to others—to his children and their mothers, to his friends, to the world of working adults and, most of all, to himself. This new chapter in his life began with "I am worthy of love and I am capable of offering that love to the world." A few years later, Steven wrote a third-person account of this important time:

> He began to look for a job. For a while, he found nothing. It was not a good time to be out of work. But one day he met a man [Edward L. Beggs] who ran a government agency ["Rites of Passage"] for the emotional and psychic rehabilitation of disturbed, angry, lost, self-destructive people. The man listened to his story, and understood. The two of them sat outside one day, as rain fell from the sky, and talked until they were soaked to the bone and shivering with suppressed excitement. The man invited him to volunteer some of his time to the agency, which he then did, and within a half-year he was being paid for his work. It wasn't much, but it was enough.
>
> He tore into his new work with great zest. He suddenly found himself surrounded by people who seemed to understand the hell he had descended into. He was eager to test his new-found insight, determinedly confident of the power of love to transform death into birth. He found resources within himself he didn't know he had. It was good, now, to be with people, to rub up against their souls; they filled him with warmth and strength. He found others who had dug themselves into dead ends, who were caught in vicious, catatonic cycles of self-destruction, and it was a positive joy to be able to say, "Look, I know where you're at. I've been there too. Stop, before you are utterly beyond reach."[21]

Within a year of his return home, Steven began planning wilderness excursions for the drug-addicted youth served by Rites of Passage. Drawing upon extensive cross-cultural research, he imagined offering these confused kids a true rite of passage in the wilderness. While the first trip was to Yosemite, thereafter he returned to the deserts of California and Nevada, again and again. This experimentation would soon become a central part of the new storyline he was creating.

Throughout his life, he often recalled the very moment when he claimed wilderness guiding as his lifework. He was crossing the Golden Gate Bridge on his way back from a chaotic trip to Death Valley with a pack of juvenile delinquents.

> Several of the kids refused the challenge of aloneness in the wilderness. Instead, they had congealed into a rat pack roaming

through the desert looking for cars to break into. One kid refused to come back. He took off with his backpack for Las Vegas, 90 miles away. Only three kids actually completed the ceremony, which involved staying alone without food in the desert for two days and two nights.

I was driving back across the Golden Gate Bridge, finally alone in the van, when it hit me like a bolt of lightning. I would do this kind of work. I would be—I was—a "vision quest guide."

Ha! Inflated with this lofty story about myself, I was fated to discover that I was nothing but a neophyte, a greenhorn of the first degree. I had just endured a week in the wilderness that could definitely be called a failure.[22]

Despite the obvious ways the trip had failed, Steven chose a storyline that exalted the great potential of what had happened, of what *could* happen. Earlier in his life he had often been mired in the slough of self-doubt, dragged down by the muck of past mistakes. He was slowly learning how to claim the blessings of his present day and the possibilities of his future. For years after, Steven often used this epiphany on the Golden Gate Bridge as an example of how people create stories about their lives, good or bad, and then turn them into self-fulfilling prophecies. "When he had this Aha!" Meredith has written, "he knew that he really wasn't a vision quest guide yet. But in saying it, claiming it, he gave it life."[23]

After years of walking backwards into the future, Steven had finally begun to turn himself around. He was now able to be grateful for where he stood, able to see his way forward, and able to tell self-fulfilling stories that were positive instead of negative. He was only just beginning to trust where he was headed.

A Lesson in Love

Lessons in self-forgiveness and gratitude can come in many forms. Some of us do this work best within an organized religion, such as going to confession in a Catholic church. Others of us need to find a more private way, such as doing some version of a "Death Lodge" during a solitary retreat. However each of us does this deeply personal work, when a significant shift inside does happen, we may find ourselves opening to the world in a new way. The remorse we have for past transgressions may deepen and become more palpable to others. When the words "please forgive me" are spoken, they may sound more authentic and may be better able to penetrate a friend's defenses. Self-forgiveness may be the very key that unlocks the door to reconciliation and redemption. Self-forgiveness—another word for self-love—deepens our capacity to love another person, which is more likely to attract a quality version of the same in return. But again, it must be emphasized, self-forgiveness is not something to be done once and once only. This is spiritual work of the hardest kind that needs to be renewed over and over.

All his life, Steven battled fiercely with the fire-and-brimstone Christianity he had inherited from his parents. Though he had tried to free himself of its grip by experimenting with most every sin, his eventual liberation would instead come from a slow-growing capacity to forgive his parents. If he could forgive himself, deadbeat dad that he had been, then he could also forgive them for their parental transgressions. Like him, they were fallible human beings. Like him, they were worthy of forgiveness, compassion, and love. Through the hard work of the Death Lodge, he was slowly learning a new way of being in the world: the way of love. Another of Steven's third-person accounts is revealing:

> Love . . . was flowing out of him, almost without his volition. It was the love that he had been unable for so many years to give to his children, to his parents, to all those around him who had populated his ghostly, crazy world. A new definition of inspiration took shape in him. It wasn't that he had to go off looking, like a frantic dog, for a bone that was buried somewhere. The muse was everywhere, corresponding to him. Gold glittered in the mouths and eyes of people. Their touch was like quicksilver. The trees moaned love, love, into the wind, and the sky was clouded with wonder. He did not have to seek the muse. She sought him, caught him, held him in her arms forever. He couldn't have escaped her if he tried.
>
> Of course, stupid fool that he was, he never quite understood, nor will he ever, how easily obtainable was the inspiration he sought. But something had reversed itself in his life. He had been lost, but now he was found. And though, many times, he felt sad and alone and deaf and blind and overwhelmed by feelings of depression and ideations of suicide, he could see

now that his portion of pain and suffering was no worse than any other human being, but that it was sufficient. The terms of his life became sufficient, and bearable. And he now possessed a magic formula: he who loves shall be filled with love.[24]

Within a year of his return from the desert, Steven began to volunteer at Marin's suicide hotline, where he and Meredith shared their weekly graveyard shift. In the dark of night, the older, but more erratic Steven often played apprentice to the younger, more stable Meredith. The lessons she had to teach were about his newfound magic formula. They were lessons about the basics of love: not sexual love (of which Steven knew plenty), but love of self and love of others.

He got in the habit of relaxing when he was around her. She was "safe." She was young, she lived with a man, she operated in another world. She existed outside his romantic concerns. He was not sexually attracted to her, though she was slim and fair and sensitive and intelligent; the odor of clear water about her. He was her friend, and she was his, once a week.

When the phone wasn't ringing and they weren't attending to its karma, the two of them talked. Though the frantic darkness pressed against the warm, pulsating womb of the suicide room, they talked—and their words became anchors cast into the other's soul. There was something in her that he instinctively trusted, something basically indefatigable, determined, open-eyed. They talked about people who called. They talked about friends. They talked about metaphysics and poetry and religion. She talked about Kant and Spinoza, he talked about Blake and Neruda. They talked about death. She was always full of questions. Sometimes he played the banjo and sang. In the very late hours, just before dawn, when the phones would go quiet for an hour or so in reverential anticipation of dawn, they would doze off, in separate beds, apart, yet strangely linked.

It was, for the two of them, a survival strategy—their way of facing death. Sometimes, death hung about the room like a grim, restless sleeplessness, and they fought it together for weary hours, with cups of coffee and backrubs. Not as though they had any chance of winning. When death struck suddenly as an unexpected phone call, it came inevitably, necessarily. One night she picked up the phone and it was a long-distance call from her stepmother in Florida, informing her that her father was dying of cancer. But she didn't cry. She didn't want to talk much about it. She was brave and sadly tragic in front of him. And then, when she was alone, she broke down and cried for the awesome life of her beautiful father, who wrote books about algae and sea life and conceived five children and loved them and cared for them and divorced their mother and went to live in Florida.[25]

By early 1975, Steven and Meredith both decided to stop their volunteer work at the hotline. On their last shift together, they wondered aloud what would become of their friendship, both expressing surprise at how important it had become. Each of them was sexually involved with another person, but over the coming months they continued to see each other as friends. Gradually they each came to realize that what they shared was more important than their other relationships. Only then did their sexual romance begin.[26]

For Meredith (and later for Steven), the story of falling in love, and later making a life commitment, was deeply entwined with the dying and death of Aldie, Meredith's father. The intensity of Aldie's final days was the fire that forged Steven and Meredith's commitment to each other. For Meredith, here were the two most important men in her life—one whom she was losing, the other whom she had just found. "So in this little slip of an overlap of my worlds," she has written, "I lost the one man who loved me unconditionally and gained a man willing and hungry to love me fully, as I was, for always—whatever madness and challenge it took us to."[27]

The day after Christmas, 1975, Meredith received a call from Ginnie, her stepmother. Aldie had fallen and was now paralyzed from the waist down. His end was near. Two days later, Meredith was on a plane to Florida; soon after Steven joined her. Meredith has written about how important that time was for Steven:

> It was at Aldie's death that Steven for the first time entered the atmosphere of what had always filled the house of Ginnie and Aldie: unguarded, deeply questioning and challenging edges of thought, mixed with acceptance, laughter, tears, creativity, honesty, openness, and love, always love. Transfer this atmosphere to Aldie's last week of dying, with about ten of their children, family, significant others, and you have the perfect environment for Steven. He entered a bliss that he longed for always, I think.

And all this mixed in with Steven's favorite topics—death, dying and love.[28]

Alden and Virginia Hine shared together what they called a "bonded love," a commitment to each other that deeply inspired Steven. He yearned for a similar relationship and, more than that, he finally believed he was capable of it. Shortly before Aldie died, Steven wrote this letter to Meredith:

> M, my feelings go beyond words, my thoughts beyond sound or form. I am proud of you and of the quality of your love and awareness. I am proud (and even jealous) of your father. As one would-be warrior to a real warrior, I say god speed. I will live my life by going inside myself until I, too, can face death, and even wish for it, as Aldie Hine has done. I will not go about unthinking the unutterable. I will seek to prepare my naïve, frightened, distracted, rudderless being to face the last and only answer to the meaning of life. I will prepare with what I have not, to enter what I know not. I am not brave, I am not understanding, I do not know how to love, I cannot say what I mean—yet I somehow live in the direct and reflected light of a star that lives within me, that would, if unchecked, flood canyons around me with pure love. For love is the star that shines in the sky that floods our canyons and arroyo secos with the invisible substance that makes things grow unto fullness of being.
>
> And so Alden Hine has grown into fullness of being. And he reflects the pure love of a star. And I will grow as he did, so help me.
>
> M, I love you. Words are so inadequate.[29]

Soon after Aldie's death, Steven and Meredith were married, and during a prolonged stay on Ithaka, one of the islands of Greece, they conceived their only child. Though this baby girl was born back in the United States, she was given the name Selene, the Greek word for moon.

The Death Lodge as Practiced Ritual

All of us are fallible human beings. Even if we have the best of intentions, we often hurt the ones we love. We say or do something we shouldn't. We fail to say or do something we should. What is unique about a bonded relationship—a commitment that is meant to last a lifetime—is not an absence of wounds, but rather a willingness to do the hard work of forgiveness and reconciliation. To keep a relationship clean and current, "I forgive you" and "you forgive me" must be exchanged month after month, year after year. Each time this is done well, the reconciliation that follows will naturally flow into "thank you" and "I love you." But if the forgiveness work is not done, or not done well, mutual gratitude and love will often dissipate. If the hurt runs especially deep, if the reconciliation work fails altogether, "goodbye" may come long before either person has died.

The work of forgiveness is easy to describe, yet so much harder to do, *especially* for a volatile person like Steven. If he and Meredith were to remain true to their bonded love, they, like any couple, would have to learn how to reconcile their differences. Steven had his own version of this universal challenge: how to bridge the huge chasm between a life of mistakes and the absolution he once had found in the wide-open spaces of the desert? For years he had seen his reflected self on the unforgiving mirrors of angry women, neglected children, and failed work. The sparse desert instead offered back a clean, undistorted image that he was slowly learning to respect. This is what drew him back to the desert, time after time, with Meredith soon joining him on most every excursion. The story of how they learned to reconcile with each other at home, day after day, is inseparable from their solitary explorations in the desert.

After five years of building a wilderness program based in the Bay Area, Steven and Meredith moved to the high desert of the Owens Valley, east of the Sierra Mountains. There in "the land of lost borders" they started a new rites of passage center called "The School of Lost Borders." Living in the desert year-round, they slowly learned to weave together their two worlds: sacred time alone in the desert and the profane life of the day-to-day. The tighter the weave, the more they understood that everything is sacred and everything is profane.

The first edition of *The Book of the Vision Quest,* published in 1980, is testimony to the first rudimentary lessons they were learning. The Death Lodge is not yet mentioned and the lessons of forgiveness, gratitude, and love are not made explicit.[30] After meeting Hyemeyohsts

Storm and hearing his Ballcourt teachings, and after putting these concepts into their own creative mill and field-testing their ideas for years, a 1988 revised edition of this book incorporated these changes, including the Death Lodge.

> Set aside a formal time to visit with the persons and events that have composed your life karma. If you feel the need, write your will. Make provisions for the disposal of your body. Commemorate the events and crises of your life from the "detached" perspective of one who is about to die. Cut the cords attached to all the exhausted placentas of your past. Now that your former life is at an end, you will die cleanly and nobly, forgiving and forgiven.[31]

Having long been incapable of maintaining balance—between wild independence and mature responsibility, between volatile anger and merciful compassion—Steven found the rite of the Death Lodge hugely transformative. Not only did it give him a way to focus on relationship issues while alone in the desert, but it also taught him a new language, including words for the giving and receiving of forgiveness. These were words he would carry back to his life with Meredith. And in turn, the two of them would offer both this language and the Death Lodge ritual to thousands of others.

Steven and Meredith considered the Death Lodge a vital part of the *severance* phase of a rite of passage, the first stage that leads up to a symbolic death. They encouraged participants preparing for a wilderness fast to have these difficult Death Lodge conversations with others, as needed, before leaving for the desert. "But most people didn't take this seriously," Meredith has written. "We saw more and more how modern people just don't do this 'making it good,' this conscious work of forgiving and apologizing."[32]

Once the participants had reached the desert, they were also encouraged to include a Death Lodge ritual as part of their solo time. The practice asked that people leave behind the confining rules of rational behavior, instead granting themselves the freedom to create this ceremony with as little self-judgment as possible.

> Find a physical place that has the feeling of "a lodge"—perhaps in a large hallow in the ground, under a tree, or in a closed-in

canyon. Mark "the doorway" with rocks or other natural objects, step inside the space, and then close "the door" behind. Sit down and wait patiently to see who comes to visit.

To each person, speak what needs to be said, perhaps even out loud. When done talking, listen for what each of them has to say in return. Briefly write in a journal, recording who came and a little about the conversations that were had. This can be exhausting work, so best not to stay in the lodge too long. If an hour or two isn't enough, close the lodge, take a break, and return later.

When finally done, give thanks to the surroundings and then close the lodge behind. If necessary, take care to dismantle all signs of the ritual.[33]

Sometimes a Death Lodge conversation in the desert leads directly to a crucial conversation with the same person back home and sometimes it doesn't. What matters most might not be the specific words spoken upon returning home but the way in which a person embodies whatever healing has happened. Ultimately, the transformative power of a Death Lodge ritual cannot be fully articulated. Without saying a word about the solitary work that was done, a person may return home and discover that old defensive patterns have shifted and the tight confines of a once-problematic relationship have loosened. Or it may become clear that the time has come to end the relationship.

To Be Blessed in Death

How each of us does the work of the Death Lodge, day after day, will likely influence the way we end our relationships as we are dying. Doing Death Lodge work doesn't require going on solitary retreats in the desert (though for some this can be a valuable practice). What it requires most is learning how to have the difficult conversations that will keep important relationships current. Some people learn how to have these conversations with a measure of grace and dignity; others try their best but never quite master them; and still others simply avoid the conversations altogether. Whatever our own approach may be, each of us is forever creating an emotional legacy that, one day, we will leave behind for our surviving family and friends. It may be a legacy of forgiveness, compassion and love; or it may be one of guilt, anger, and resentment.

For Steven, the central lesson of the Death Lodge was not to wait until he was dying to start healing the wounds of his most important relationships. It took him more than half his life to learn this lesson, but once he had, he and Meredith would share that teaching with many. More important than telling others, though, was doing their relationship work together, right up to the very end of Steven's life.

"To be blessed in life, one must learn to die," says the first half of an old medieval prayer.[34] This was certainly true for Steven. He didn't begin to open to life's blessings until after he began learning how to die symbolically.

"To be blessed in death, one must learn to live."[35] Because physical death is often unpredictable, the second half of this prayer may be harder to realize. But by learning basic lessons about self-forgiveness, gratitude, and love, Steven had done his best to invite in a blessed death.

Second Home Visit

January 29: Wow! as the old hippies say. This afternoon I took half of the prescribed dose of morphine. So good to feel relaxed, to allow breath to come more automatically. A thousand, thousand galaxies and stars, dear doctor, for your crown!

It is still difficult to believe in the efficacy of medication, knowing it is nothing more than a nice band-aid. Illusion, as the Buddhists say. Death is still waiting for me—but I think she has had to back up a few months and momentarily hide herself.

And yes, doc, if you must know, I love you. Okay, enough of that.[1]

March 25: So here I come from "off the grid" to ask for delectable favors, such as prescriptions for the restricted drug called oxygen and the honey powder at the heart of the flower called morphine sulphate. Morpheus!

But what I really need at the moment is a prescription for continued rehab training, downright physical, agonizing training, at a first-rate physical therapy facility, preferably Marin-style, and close enough, via the traffic labyrinth, to conveniently reach three times a week. The six week pulmonary rehab program has been a sweet and enlightening time for both of us. I need more. I'm not ready to stop fighting, even though it would be easy to just let go.

Even more than these delectable bon mots, I—we—want to spend time in your physical presence, no topic verboten. If you had a day off from your birthing work, we would love to have you make a "home visit" to us in this beautiful house in Mill Valley, where we live now and probably until some unrevealed time. The house belongs to M's parents and the Little family, although only mom and dad are living here now. Dad is 91. Mom is 80. Lessons here, eh?

I am well, doc. With help from you, morphine sulfate, and Spirit, I withdrew from my beloved scotch and am now living at sea level with my beautiful woman. We arise in the morning to the singing of birds.

We love you, even though we hardly know you.[2]

— Steven Foster, emails to the author

Second Home Visit

Saturday, April 5

I drove slowly through the small mountainside village of Mill Valley, its streets lined with trendy shops catering to the hip and well heeled of Marin County. The stores gave way to a row of homes, which soon began to spread out, making room for a forest of old-growth redwoods. It was a sunny day in early spring, but once I entered the dark of the forest I had to turn on the headlights to see my way forward.

I felt a nervous anticipation rattling inside my chest, a fluttering sensation as if I'd had too much coffee and not enough to eat. I flashed back to a lesson from anatomy lab years ago. The solar plexus is a network of nerves in front of the aorta and behind the breast bone, which sends impulses out to the abdominal organs. That plexus of nerves was now firing away constantly, like telephone wires on a Christmas day.

Why all the anxiety? I thought I'd sorted this all out in Joshua Tree.

Despite some cold nights, the trip to the desert had been a great success—both for the group and for me. Though the solo fast was only twenty-four hours, many of the other people had gone deep inside themselves and the stories afterward had bonded the group. For my own solo, I had carried into the desert the internal battle between being Steven's physician and being his student. For hours on end, a near-constant dialogue between the two had spilled out of my head and into my journal. One voice was the physician who prided himself in being responsible and giving; the other, the student who wanted to engage with the teacher, even though he feared he might be seen as groveling. Their disparate ways seemed irreconcilable, until a small epiphany came while I lay half-asleep the next morning. *Lead with service.* Simple as that. *Let go of role definition and lead with service.*

I reached my destination, a driveway with a sign by it that read "The Littles," marking the home of Meredith's parents.

Lead with service. I repeated these words a few times as I got out of the car. *Don't worry about roles, just lead with service.*

Walking down a steep, curving driveway through a grove of redwoods, I recalled an email from Steven, written in response to my own report about the desert trip.

> Dearest doc, dearest friend, so good to hear of your travels to Joshua Tree—fun, adventure, memory, self-forgiveness, signs of healing and dying, doctors and nurses willing to cross, with their own myths, into the vortex of perfection. So the soul of perfection is a Dark University with a library in which its rare book collection contains a perfect phrase that must always be repeated again.
>
> Doctor and/or student. Interesting question. Don't we do this for each other anyway? Do you need a diagnosis or a prescription? You can count on me.[3]

Steven's invitation was clear. Bring "all of me" to each visit, be it doctor, student, or friend. Even with my new mantra about service, I wasn't sure whether I was ready for where that might take me.

Before reaching to open a wooden gate at the end of the driveway, I repeated one last time, *Lead with service.* Even with this clear intention, when I stepped through the portal, the solar plexus began firing away double-time.

I found myself in a large, open courtyard: swirling circles of red brick at my feet, a large patch of blue sky above, and a most unusual house across the courtyard. Arching redwood beams, rescued from a dismantled highway bridge in Ukiah, supported a roof covered with red volcanic rock and walls made mostly of glass. The redwood of the beams, the red brick of the courtyard, and the red rock of the roof all blended with the surrounding forest of redwoods, pines, and oaks, intentionally blurring the line between man and nature.

This is more than a building, I told myself. *This is not just a house.*

I knocked on the door and introduced myself to an older woman who greeted me with her alert eyes and engaging smile.

"I'm Liz," she said, "Meredith's mother." She ushered me into the house, displaying a vibrancy that belied her eighty years. "Scott is your name? How wonderful to meet a doctor still willing to do a home visit."

I commented about the unusual house, which prompted a brief tour. Designed in the early 1960s by Daniel Liebermann, Berkeley architect and former student of Frank Lloyd Wright, the house had been built for Liebermann's parents. Liz and Meredith's stepfather, Phil, bought it in 1966 when they moved their family from Minnesota to the Bay Area.

Liz led me outside to a flight of stairs that led down to an add-on unit wedged against the hillside. "This is where Meredith lived when she was a teenager," she explained, "along with her two sisters."

After saying our goodbyes, I began climbing down the stairs. Then it came to me: *This place is not merely a house. This is a home. Once home for Meredith and her family. Now home for Steven and Meredith. Steven's last home.*

Meredith greeted me at the door with a welcoming smile, though our embrace was still a bit awkward. In such a short time, she and Steven had allowed me deep into their lives, but as Steven's latest email had said, "We hardly know you."

Before ushering me in, she warned me she'd be leaving soon to run some errands. "Really just an excuse to leave you alone with Steven," she explained. "The type of conversation you offer is something he doesn't get much of these days."

I followed her through the entrance foyer into a single room big enough to hold a large bed, a table cluttered with a computer, piles of books and papers, and a muted television tuned to a basketball game. The bed, where Steven was sitting, faced a wall of low-lying bookshelves, over which large windows offered a panoramic view to the forest.

Swinging his legs from the bed to the floor, a clean-shaven Steven stood up. Though oxygen tubing tethered him to a nearby tank, he walked a few important steps to meet me halfway. Our faces met with equally big smiles, though his greeting seemed more passionate, more urgent than mine. *Was this his usual way?* I wondered. *Or is life too short now to waste time being hesitant?*

As we embraced, I felt a quiver just beneath my breastbone. *The solar plexus again,* I thought. But the feeling was different this time, more a warm glow than an anxious firing. *A special connection made physical.* As our bodies separated, I acknowledged the connection by placing my hand on Steven's chest, rubbing it with a few slow circles.

How appropriate, I thought, remembering when I had first used this hand-on-chest gesture. My first time in a desert base-camp as assistant guide, I unconsciously started doing it as a way of expressing the uncommon intimacy of the work. Later at home, I found myself using it more consciously, but only during very special moments with friends.

Stepping back from Steven, I looked at his black T-shirt, right where I had been rubbing. "I'm only wearing black," it said, "until they make something darker."

"That's quite the shirt you have there, Steven."

"Isn't it great?" He grinned as he tugged at the bottom corners of the shirt. "It's a gift from Gigi Coyle, founder and director of the Dark Institute. You've heard of the Institute, I presume."

"Absolutely." I had heard about the mythic university from Gigi herself. People qualified for membership, she had explained, only if they had spent enough time exploring their own dark night of the soul. "Though I haven't submitted my official application," I told Steven, "I think my experiences growing up should qualify me. And if that's not enough, then the years in residency will certainly clinch it."

"That's good." He stepped back to sit on the bed. "Can't imagine a hospice doctor who doesn't have a special degree in Depression and Darkness."

Meredith walked around from behind me, turned the television off, and took a spot off to the side, leaning against the wall. She stood suspended on one leg, the other bent, looking as graceful as an egret.

After bantering briefly about the basketball game, I asked Steven about his recent bout of chest pain. The sudden onset of a sharp pain had worried Meredith enough to wonder whether he should go to the hospital. After she had called me, I had arranged for him to get a chest X-ray and some blood work done at the nearest facility, but when I checked for results later he hadn't gone in.

"The pain is lots better," said Steven, rubbing his own chest wall. "Not nearly as bad as the last day or two. I don't think I'll be kicking the bucket too soon. Not today anyway."

"Sure had me worried," Meredith said more seriously, placing both feet firmly on the ground. She explained how he had kept refusing to go to the hospital, even if just for some tests. Steven grimaced at her sweetly when she finished. Meredith smiled back.

A yellow flag, I thought. *Would Steven ever be willing to go to the hospital?*

After a thorough telling of his chest pain story, I did a physical exam. The key finding was tenderness on his chest wall where one of the ribs attaches to the breastbone.

"Costochondritis," I said. "Inflammation of the rib cartilage. Nothing serious, though it can hurt like hell. You probably injured yourself while coughing." I explained the roles of morphine and anti-inflammatories, such as ibuprofen. Meredith, forever the nurse, inquired about dosing and frequency, which led to further questions about Steven's other meds.

"Great, that helps," said Meredith. "Time now to leave you two alone." She kissed Steven and then briefly placed her hand on my shoulder as she walked by. "He's all yours."

"That woman is a miracle," said Steven after Meredith was gone. "Anything I need, she's right there. Often before I even know I need it. She's my greatest blessing and my greatest curse."

"Why a curse?"

"We're so attached, I wonder if she'll ever let go of me. She's put so much of herself into keeping me alive." He described her endless capacity to help: frequent small meals, letters and emails, errands, organizing the work of each day. "But it's even more than just the tasks. She's constantly looking to give me one more reason to want to live." A look of agitation slowly distorted his face.

"I've been a terrible beast to her. So many times. Too many times. Yet she continues to love me in this incredible way. To love me while still remaining true to herself. Now that's a miracle. I tell you, doc, the inescapable fact of her love will forever confound me. It's the greatest mystery of my life."

He turned away, staring out at the forest, lost in thought.

"So, yeah," he continued, "I worry. M has thrown so much into keeping me alive. Makes me wonder. Will she be able to just let me die?"

I waited, wanting to be sure he was done. "Steven, makes me think of someone I once took care of." I told him about Richard, a young man who had died of AIDS fifteen years earlier, when I was just starting out as a doctor. "I remember telling him and his partner both, 'Soon there'll be room enough for only two people. Then, room enough just for one.'"

"Bulls-eye, doc. I'd love to whittle this big, crazy life of ours down to just the two of us. The two of us plus family. But that's impossible."

He sat up a little straighter, leaning forward. His mind was coming alive, while his body was struggling to keep up.

"And then comes the even harder task." He stared directly at me. "Room enough only for one. Yep, I worry about her. Will she be able to let go of this ol' beast? For twenty-five years straight, save a few days, we've shared nearly every hour together. Along the way, we've made a great myth of ourselves. Always together. Never 'just-Steven.' Or 'just-Meredith.' Always 'Steven-and-Meredith.' How do we ever divide that in half? How do we let just the Steven-half die?"

"That's the greatest test of love. Can Meredith love you enough to finally let you go, to release you to what has to come?"

The old hospice teaching about completing a relationship came to mind, though the first two steps about forgiveness didn't seem necessary for them.

"When the time comes," I added, "will you both be able to say to each other, 'Thank you, I love you, and goodbye'?"

Steven shifted his position in bed, again staring outside. I waited, but no response came. Eventually he looked back at me, though still silent.

"Steven, say more about this big, crazy life of yours. What has it been like trying to whittle that down?"

"Well, except for this June training, I'm pretty much done with wilderness work. We've left that in good hands—work for others to do. Living now is mostly about one-on-one relationships. But damn, there are still so many of those. It's why I did my road trip awhile back. What I called 'my Death Lodge journey.'"

"Tell me about it."

"A month-long road trip in January. A road show that played to some mixed reviews." He described his itinerary, driving around to visit many of his most important people. First his mother in the desert, east of Los Angeles. Then Los Angeles and San Diego. Next, the Bay Area for the largest group. Last, Oregon and Washington. "I did all of it alone. Had to be alone. I needed to know, one last time, if I could get by without Meredith constantly rescuing me."

"One last solo journey."

"That's right. Me and my oxygen tank and a beat-up Oldsmobile. A car as old as me. It had broken down the week before and would only drive with the automatic transmission stuck in second. It's a miracle we made it as far as we did."

"You mentioned some mixed reviews. What was that like?"

"Remember, this was my Death Lodge journey. I wanted to sit with each person one last time. Tell 'em I was dying. Tell 'em I wanted to come clean. Forgive and be forgiven. Love and be loved. You see, that's dying's greatest gift, love. For God's sake, love. Love for people. Love for this earth. The closer you get to the end, the clearer that becomes. As clear as the desert air after a heavy rain."

"So let me guess. A few people weren't ready to go straight to forgiveness."

"Damn right. What was so clear to me, wasn't so clear for everyone else. Some people just didn't get it. This was it. Our last chance. Our last chance in person, anyway."

"Maybe they didn't want to believe you really are dying."

"You're probably right. The only obvious sign that something's wrong is this tube crammed up my nose." He swatted the oxygen line with his hand. "And they've been seeing this for years. And for years we've all tried to ignore what's been happening. We stopped talking about how the old mountain man is slowly fading to black. How the sun is nearly down and the light's going fast."

From his bedstand, he picked up an inhaler. After a few practice breaths, he gave himself a couple of puffs. He sat still for a time, waiting for the drug to open his airways a few extra microns.

"But dammit, they should've seen me when I caught that swamp virus in Washington. Nearly killed me." By the end of the trip, he explained, he could drive only a couple of hours a day and had to take large detours to avoid the thin air of the mountains.

"Steven, when someone can't see that you're dying, can't find a way to forgive, what do you do then?"

"Well, then, you just have to forgive yourself, which ain't always easy. Like I said, the more I dance with the Dark Goddess, the easier it gets to forgive other people. But me? I'm a hard one to let off the hook."

"Not so from this side, Steven. Seems to me, you're an easy one to love."

Steven moaned softly, eyes cast to the floor. "Doctor Feelgood," he said, looking up. "That's what we'll have to call you, Doc Feelgood."

"Don't be so sure. I'm also a master of the difficult conversation. Always willing to go to the dark places."

"If you're the one leading, I'm willing to follow."

"Okay then. Tell me more about this big, bulky life of yours. What you were describing earlier. With that Death Lodge journey done, why's your life still out of control?"

"People. Countless people who need something. Words of advice. Words of support. Words of wisdom. It's love karma. The result of this work we do. The work we've chosen to do. Day after day, year after year. Listening to people's stories, supporting them, encouraging them, loving them."

He paused to catch his breath. For a moment, he looked weak and vulnerable.

"So many people, doc. All coming to me as if I had honey dripping from my lips."

"But it is honey." I smiled.

"Hah!" he scoffed.

"So tell me about all these demands. What do they look like?"

"Okay, doc." He pointed to the table behind me where his computer sat. "Sitting on that pile of papers is a card from a man who trained with us years ago. He's asked me to write him a letter of recommendation for some new venture of his." Steven briefly described the fellow: a good man, a gentle man, but someone whose life had been especially hard. "The details of his story may not be important to you, but for him, those details are everything. And if I'm to hear his story, if I'm to help him move that story forward, then those details have got to be important to me, too."

"Just like being a doctor. Needing to really show up for people, even if sometimes it's at your own expense."

"Yep, must be similar." He considered that for a moment. "So here's this guy trying to make a new start and somehow he thinks a letter from this ol' fart is going to help him out. He needs *me*. Or so he thinks. So what am I to do with that? Say 'no'?" He motioned with his arms as if he was passing a great load onto someone else. "Or do I just give all the cards, letters, and emails over to Meredith?"

A little breathless, he stopped talking. After a few deep inhales, precious oxygen settled deeper into his lungs, seeping into the bloodstream and into his brain.

"Damn, doc, I sound like a sniveling creep. But there it is. I'm trapped in my own hell, a special hell of my own making. All I wanna do is love people, but I've got no energy for it. Not anymore. So poor Meredith, she's left to do most of the work."

"Steven, sounds like it's time to start shutting the door on your Death Lodge. First complete your relationships with this great legion of well-wishers. And after that, only let in your inner circle."

"Yeah, yeah, yeah," he said, moving his arms about, signaling for me to back off. He was still easily drained, but his recovery time seemed faster. *Rehab must be helping,* I told myself.

"Doc, we didn't call ourselves 'The School of Lost Borders' for nothing. No borders, no limits." He described how so many of their early teachers, from Storm to Grandpa Raymond to Sun Bear, had taught them to be available for whomever came, even people showing up in the middle of the night. "Those night visits used to make our kids crazy. But this has been our lifework. Our giveaway."

"Whoa, Steven, now there's a recipe guaranteed to leave you burnt and crispy. Sounds as bad as residency training, maybe worse. Actually, let me give you the same advice I've been offering to young doctors for years. After you leave residency, you've got to learn to say 'no' so that your 'yes' still means something."

"Hey, doc, you gotta do what you gotta do."

"Right you are. And now you gotta do something different. You've got to. However much time you have left—days, weeks, months, or years—your world is going to get smaller. If you want to say a real 'yes' to your family, you've got to be saying 'no' to those other folks. You've got to be ruthless."

"Ooooh," he groaned, his eyes widening. "Ruthless! Do you know what the origin of that word is?"

I shook my head 'no.' *The English professor,* I reminded myself.

"Ruth-less. Without ruth. Without pity. You're asking me to have no pity. Nope, I don't think so."

His persistent desire to serve surprised me, touched me. Still, I was on a mission. I refused to waver.

"If that's what it takes, well then, no pity it has to be."

I heard a touch of self-righteous anger in my voice. Three years of residency, and all the hard work that followed, had beaten the lesson of self-care into me. Ruthless self-care. Caring for yourself *has* to matter as much as caring for others. Otherwise, you stop caring for either.

"Steven, how else will Meredith and your family get what they deserve? How else will *you* get what *you* deserve?"

He averted my eyes.

"Oh, Steven. Dear sweet Steven. Forgive me. I know I'm lecturing. But I just want to wrap you up and protect you from all these folks." His face slowly changed from old man to little boy. "You know, I've seen it over and over. For so many people, especially those who have spent a lifetime caring for others, the hardest part of dying is learning to receive. It's now time for other people to protect you, to care for you. Time for you to be the one receiving the love."

Leaning over, looking at the floor, he shook his head from side to side and moaned—a guttural noise coming from the deepest part of his Swiss cheese lungs. He looked up and wiped some tears away.

"Promise me, doc. When there's room left for only a few people, you'll be one of them."

"I give you my word, Steven. If it's within my powers, I'll be there."

"I have something for you, doc. Consider it payment for the work ahead."

With fingers trembling slightly, he picked a small copper coin off his bedside table and handed it to me. The coin, about the size of a penny, had on its top side a large "1," with "pfennig" written below in smaller letters.

Steven recounted the story of his German friends giving him the penny after singing him the ferryman song. He added a brief description of Charon, boatman to the Underworld.

"The River Styx isn't far ahead. When it's time for the final crossing, doc, I want you there at the helm."

A long silence settled between us. This time it was me who looked out the window. As if for the first time, I saw the cathedral of trees that surrounded us. It redefined the space of the bedroom to a much greater size, a much greater height.

A place of safety and serenity, I thought. *A good place to die. And I'll be here when the time comes.*

The magic of the moment eventually faded, leaving an empty space in the conversation. We began filling in the gap with small talk and, soon after, Meredith returned. She took her same place, leaning against the wall behind Steven.

Time for one more doctor task, I decided. With Meredith back, it was time to investigate the yellow flag I had recognized earlier in the visit.

"Back to the subject of borders, Steven. Yesterday you chose not to go to the hospital. Is the entrance to a hospital a permanent border, something you'll never cross again?"

Together we considered where it was Steven wanted to draw the line. No more hospitals? No more E.R. visits? No more X-rays and blood tests? No more antibiotics? He said a definite "no" to the first two, but reserved the right to say "yes" to the others.

"There's no cure for what I got, doc. Sure, if I got sick, you might get an infection under control and that's worth a try. But only to a point. Fact is . . ." He stopped and looked back to Meredith. "Fact is, I'm still dying."

Meredith didn't flinch.

"Sure, I'm also living. Especially with this rehab program, I can feel my strength returning. But even with that, I might still get a pneumonia that would knock me to the ground. And if I do, you won't see me rushing back to the hospital. That'll be time for stepping onto the Great Ballcourt. For dancing before the Lords and Ladies of Death. Maybe they'll grant me another day, maybe they won't."

I reviewed his choices, confirming where exactly he stood. He was unwavering. No more hospitals, except for a blood draw or a simple X-ray. Even those seemed unlikely.

"Here's another concern, Steven. A bit of a problem, though not insurmountable." I explained how his new home was almost an hour from where I lived and even farther from my hospital and clinic. If he decided he wanted to get some tests done, he would be getting them from a medical community that didn't know me. Even if what he wanted was limited—a simple test or two—I couldn't pretend to be the best person to provide that. "What do you think if we get a local doctor involved?" I asked. "Someone who could get you what you need here in Marin."

"But you're the doctor I want," he blurted out. "I don't wanna lose you."

I heard something of the little boy in him again, so I did my best to reassure him. "If you want me, you'll still have me coming here. Just as often, either way. Remember, no borders. Doesn't matter if I'm coming here as doctor, student, or friend. Just that I show up."

I cringed inside. *Am I repeating the same mistake again?* Ten years before, I had tried to be both doctor and friend to the same person, only to have it nearly ruin me. *Just lead with service,* I reminded myself.

"Hey doc, you okay?"

"Yep, I'm fine." And truthfully I was. Now, in the middle of the visit, the mantra about service did point the way forward.

I explained to Steven about my new boundary issue: instead of struggling to be both doctor and student, this one was about being both doctor and friend.

"This is the School of Lost Borders, doc. Lose them borders, I say." He swept a backhand volley big enough for a tennis match.

"Of course," I said, "that would be the lesson you'd have to teach, wouldn't it?"

We both laughed.

"Come on, doc, just remember what you said in your email. It's not about specific roles. It's about service."

"Yep, lead with service. So that begs the question, what will serve *you* most? Having another doctor involved or not?" We talked awhile about options. Meredith, more than Steven, saw the advantage of having a local doctor involved, just in case. We left it that I would do some research and get back to them with a list of names.

"Seems like we've traded places," said Steven. "You want me to set more limits, reestablish some lost borders. And you, you need to be tearing some down."

"So we meet in the middle, Steven. Right?"

"Right you are, Scott." It was the first time I could recall him using my first name.

After more small talk, Steven eventually took the role of guide and teacher, as he had done at the end of the previous visit. The hospice fast was his first topic.

"First time we saw you, doc, you said you were looking to bridge the world of hospice and rites of passage. M and I want to support you stepping into that in a big way."

He offered an inspired monologue about the vision quest as a way to practice dying. The more he talked, the more energy he seemed to generate—his face opening, his arms and hands gesturing, his voice filling with passion. His words peaked with a quote from Plato: "True devotees of self-knowledge practice nothing but learning how to die."

"And that's what we've been helping people to do for years. Who would benefit from that practice more than people who actually work with the dying?"

"And who better to offer it to them than you?" added Meredith. "You're both a hospice physician and a wilderness guide."

Again their offer was like a drug, but this time its effects were not so overpowering. No great rush this time, but also no anxious after-effects.

"After all you've done for us," said Meredith, "are you capable of receiving something in return?"

Yes, I thought to myself, *that's the important question! If I'm here to serve, is it okay if I get something back?*

I tried to explain to them that, while being a doctor or a wilderness guide can be similar, they're not the same. The doctor-patient relationship is inherently unequal. Ill people usually are vulnerable, while doctors often have information or access to treatment that gives them special power. With that power comes a special responsibility, which is why it's so crucial to lead with service.

"Steven, I think you're right about me needing to lose some borders. About learning to let 'all of me' show up. But still, as your doctor, I have to lead with what will serve you."

"And what will serve other people," offered Meredith.

"That's right, doc." Steven continued without missing a beat. "If we co-create something for hospice folks, it won't be for you and it won't be for us. It'll be for them."

Again I stared out at the redwoods, mulling this over. I heard the loud song of a single bird. She was repeating the same penetrating whistle over and over. *Has she just started singing,* I wondered? *Or am I only now hearing her song?*

"Okay, service it is," I said. "Lead with service and let the roles define themselves."

"Right on, doc."

We talked a while longer about what another hospice fast might look like. First the how of it, a little bit about when and where, then whom to contact.

Steven continued as teacher, but the topics started shifting at a quicker pace. First he asked questions about my own struggles with dark times and then about my years of doing solitary retreats. That led to a more focused inquiry about time spent alone in nature.

Unlike during the first visit, I enjoyed the enthusiasm of his questions. What else could I do but answer him truthfully? Here was a man, like so few others, who would settle for nothing less than his doctor showing up as a full person. He wanted to see the warts, the failings, and the shadow, as much as the love and the light.

"So it all comes clear why we connect," said Steven in summary. "You're a member of the Dark Institute, check. You've spent lots of time alone in nature, check. You've fasted several times, check. You feel called to guide others, check. You're even a writer, check."

"And I share an obsession with death as a teacher."

"Major check!" His smile was now as big as it had been all day.

"A match made in heaven. Or is it a match made in hell, the hell of your dying?"

"Heaven and hell," said Steven. "What's heaven one day can seem like hell the next. But it's always the same place. The world just reflects back what you bring to it."

Steven picked up a book from his bedside table, opened to the first page and wrote a few lines, then handed it to me. "The German pfennig was payment for services to be rendered. Consider this to be a gift."

I looked at the cover and the book's title: *We Who Have Gone Before: Memory and an Old Wilderness Midwife.*

"There's another book on the way soon," he explained, "the one we showed you last visit. This one came out last year."

I opened the book to the first page and read the words he had written.

> *For Scott,*
> *With the deepest,*
> *fullest, widest gratitude*
> *for your precious life and work.*
> *With love, Steven.*

I closed the book and stared at it for a long time, fingering its slick, glossy cover. Again I felt that warm glow inside my chest. "Thank you, Steven. Thank you so much."

"You're welcome. No, you're more than just welcome. You've earned those words. But as for the book itself, I offer it as part of an exchange. If you'd be willing, I'd love a copy of your own book."

Surprised, I scanned my brain for any memory of having told him about it.

"Of course you did," he reminded me. "You mentioned it during your first visit. *A Long Way Home,* wasn't that the title?"

"That's right. Guess I did tell you about it. The writing of that book was crucial for me, a real source of healing."

"Finding a way to tell your own story usually is. So does the book have a subtitle?"

"Memoirs of a Medical Heretic."

"Ah, so you're a subversive, too. Shoulda known. One more reason why we get along so well."

After promising to mail him a copy of my book, I felt my neck starting to stiffen. I tried to stretch it out as best I could.

"Doc, you're looking tired," said Steven.

"Suppose I am. Looks like you've outlasted me today."

"Next time we meet halfway," he insisted. "And maybe for not so long a time."

"Now there's another role reversal. I'm the one fading and you're the one coming to the rescue."

"Like you said, Scott, just lead with service. You need a doctor and I'm there."

"And I'll do the same for you, my friend."

After hugs and goodbyes with the two of them, I started up the stairs.

"Hey, Scott," Steven called out.

Half-way up, I turned around.

"Next time, remind me to tell you all about my life as a gangster."

"Right, Steven. I'll do that."

Part 3

Purpose Circle

Decision road does not stop . . . at {the death lodge,} the little house at the edge of the village. It leads to the purpose circle on the mountain, to the dying place, where the initiate goes beyond the realm of the living to the hope of birth. There she will stand alone.[1]

— Steven Foster and Meredith Little, *The Roaring of the Sacred River*

You go alone to the exact place in which you have chosen to die. Now you are completely without physical assistance. You have crossed the boundary of rational control. Now you are at the mouth of the death passage that leads to birth. All day you pray and sing to those powers and presences in your life, asking them to help you die. Slowly, night falls. In the darkness you pray and wait. The death passage lies dead ahead, where the karmic monsters of your former life lurk in illusory shadows. Here in the circle of your life's purpose, you hold true to that which you sense is your destiny.[2]

— Steven Foster with Meredith Little, *The Four Shields*

Purpose Circle

Integrity vs. Despair

Imagine again that you have consciously stepped onto Decision Road, a path that leads from the Death Lodge onto the Purpose Circle. Here is your final stop on the way to the Great Ballcourt. The Purpose Circle is a place for reviewing your past so you can step fully into the present—the present moment of your dying. A religious person might think: *There I will meet my Maker.* An agnostic or atheist might ask: *What have I made of my life?*

The work of the Purpose Circle begins by bringing closure to the life you have lived. This can be done in many ways. With advance directives, you can make clear what you want done with your physical body before and after your death. With a legal will, you can distribute all your worldly possessions as you see fit. In an ethical will, you can bequeath your values to those you love, writing down for them your successes and your regrets, your beliefs and your doubts, your instructions and your wishes. Inside a memory box, you can collect mementos of your life so that those who love you will more easily remember you in the years to come. And in written form, you can leave behind a description of the memorial service you want held after you die.*

In the Purpose Circle you also do a major life review. Some of this can be done with family and friends, asking them to sit with you while you look at old photographs, tell old stories, and sing old songs. When you give shape to life memories in this way, you behold them more clearly. Your life is like a collection of old movie reels, some made a few years ago, others made decades ago. With the help of friends and family, you run some of these movies one last time, reminding yourself of all that you have seen and been and done. You do this not to hold onto them more tightly but to let them go.

* See Resources, page 169 for more information about advance directives, wills, ethical wills, memory boxes, and memorial services.

Though friends and family can help you do some of this work, ultimately the Purpose Circle is a place for your own personal reckoning. If you believe in a Higher Power, this accounting will likely be done with your God; otherwise, this final summation will be done alone, within yourself. Either way, you may find yourself asking some of life's biggest questions. *Within my own value system, was the life I lived "good enough?" Where did I find my greatest purpose? How did I give my life meaning?* Erik Erikson has named the challenge of this final stage of life "Ego Integrity vs. Despair."[3] As you reflect on all that you've done, are you filled with a deep contentment? Or are you haunted by feelings of failure and regret? Whichever it is, at the center of your own Purpose Circle you will either stand alone or stand before your God, declaring one last time: *This is what I made of my life, and this is who I am.*

The measure of a person's life is seldom to be found in a single purpose; most of us give ourselves over to a variety of endeavors, creating an array of "movies." For many people, life's central purpose is found in creating a family: both raising children and excelling at a job that will support them. For artists, the creative act becomes a major focus. For the service-oriented, caring for people in need or fighting for a righteous cause can be important. For the spiritually-minded, following a chosen faith or maintaining a regular practice may become central to their lives. From these and other pursuits, each of us selects different ways of finding meaning and purpose. Standing in your final Purpose Circle, you may look back on all that you've done and ask yourself: *Did I choose well? Did I give myself fully to what mattered most? Was mine a life well-lived?*

Even if your life was mostly good, inevitably you will have to face some monsters, old regrets that never quite faded. None of us has all of our prayers answered, all of our dreams realized, all of our goals achieved. Just as you exchanged forgiveness with others in the Death Lodge, you may also need to seek forgiveness within yourself—for some of what you did, and for some of what you didn't do. Some people will do this by telling themselves: *I forgive me.* Others will pray to a Higher Power: *God, please forgive me.* Still others may need to find a way of saying: *God, I forgive you.*

The universal search for purpose and meaning often becomes

more frustrating as a person nears the end of life. Purpose is so often tied directly to action, as in the phrase *purposeful activity;* and yet as the life force is draining away, it may become increasingly difficult *to do* anything. When you have reached the final months of your own life, more and more you will likely need others *to do* for you. *Now that I'm so incapacitated,* you might ask yourself, *how can I be of any use?* If you are blessed to have family and friends willing to care for you, one possible answer is learning to accept their love and support. If you are fortunate to be held, fed, and bathed in your final days, remember that a gift of this magnitude can become a reciprocal act. To the people who offer you this special care, you may be giving back the tender memory of how they loved you during your final days. Perhaps this will be your final legacy, your last giveaway. As Erikson wrote, "healthy children will not fear life if their elders have integrity enough not to fear death."[4]

How your own last days will actually unfold is impossible to predict. Maybe yours will be a slow dying, with you surrounded by people you love. Or perhaps instead you will survive to an advanced old age, outliving all the people who might have cared for you. Or maybe you will die suddenly, your final Purpose Circle reduced to a quick flash through past memories and regrets. Would any of these scenarios rob your life of its meaning?

Truth is, each of us is creating a personal legacy every day that we are alive. What ultimately gives meaning to life is not merely the way we die—the final chapter of a lifestory. Each and every chapter is important. Both the inevitability of death and the uncertainty of life challenge us all not to postpone asking and answering big questions about purpose and meaning. To bring this all into focus, we might ask ourselves: *If I died today, suddenly and without warning, what would be my legacy?*

Becoming Twice-Born

In the words of William James, "mankind's common instinct for reality . . . has always held the world to be essentially a theatre for heroism."[5] A half-century later, Campbell would call this universal search for meaning and purpose "the hero's journey."[6] The word *hero* can have several meanings, with the phrases "a mythic hero" or "the hero of a story" usually being reserved for someone who is singularly special. Campbell suggests, however, that all of us are called to be "heroes" within the terms and values of our own lives. Perhaps the best mark of personal heroism is not astounding courage or accomplishments, but authentic self-expression and devotion to whatever unique calling a person discovers.

For people living long ago in a small, contained community, the ways of becoming "a hero" were well defined. Young children of a tribe or village were taught the same group mythology: a collective story that guided each of them, unimpeded, from the cradle to the grave. In return for surrendering to this group myth, most everyone was given both a place within the community and the possibility of becoming a smaller-scale hero by serving the larger group. As just one example, for centuries, many people in Europe, America and elsewhere have inherited a Judeo-Christian mythology. Though many variations exist, the basic mythology holds that each of us is born into this world as an act of God, and if we serve Him with dignity—if we marry, procreate, and work within and for our faith community—we each will be granted a place of respect, both on earth and in heaven.

If no competing worldviews are brought in by visitors, books, newspapers, radio, television, or the internet, an inherited mythology can remain unquestioned for generations. In the modern world, however, few isolated communities still exist. We live instead in a complex, interconnected global village, where the flashing neon of the new is superimposed on the weathered structures of the old. We are constantly bombarded by a cacophony of voices: parents and peers, churches and governments, doctors and lawyers, poets and movie stars, wise men and lunatics. With so many of these outside challenges, more and more people have questioned, rejected, or drifted away from the group mythology that they inherited.

In the modern world, the search for meaning and purpose has increasingly become a private and personal life journey, including for many people who continue to practice their inherited faith. Borrowing from Joseph Campbell:

> The problem of mankind today, therefore, is precisely the opposite to that of men in the comparatively stable periods of

those great co-ordinating mythologies . . . Then all meaning was in the group, in the great anonymous forms, none in the self-expressive individual; today no meaning is in the group—none in the world: all is in the individual.[7]

Even in these modern times, an individual's search for heroism must begin within a group mythology, whether it is one that is religious or one that is secular and scientific. That group myth serves as the semiconscious foundation upon which each of us will build a personal lifestory. But even before we reach adulthood, that inherited myth will be challenged from outside by so much truth and so much madness. How do we make sense of all the competing voices? How do we avoid simplistically dividing the world into good and bad, right and wrong? The answer, according to Campbell, is for each person to find and express an authentic voice, a deeper inner wisdom. And to do that, he says, each of us must die to the group mythology we inherited so that we may then become twice-born.[8] For some people, this will mean holding onto the worldview or religion that they inherited, but transforming it into something that is more personally alive and resonant. For others, finding an authentic voice will be possible only after rejecting much of what was handed down to them.

For Steven, a radical breaking-away from Christianity was his only way forward. He had inherited a fundamentalist worldview that was inadequate for his dynamic personality and the vibrant times into which he was born. Still, in its own limited way, that mythology did serve him. Most importantly, it taught him about the miracle of life and the mystery of death. It also gave him a good start in life: a reasonably happy childhood, an education at a Christian college, and a career as a university professor. Where the mythology failed him most, however, was in giving him an image of the universe that was too one-dimensional, and a moral order that was too rigid.

The story of Steven's early adulthood—a quickly dissolving first marriage, suicidal thoughts, divorce and remarriage, experimentation with mind-expanding drugs, and loss of his professional identity and family—can all be read as the tale of a young man dying, fully and painfully, to the Christian mythology he had been given. For Steven to become twice-born, his first life would have to come to a dramatic end.

Healing the Split

In a world where all meaning is to be found in the solitary and the personal, many people will follow a path that is convoluted (even dangerous, as Steven's story reveals). Returning to Campbell:

> But there [in the individual] the meaning is absolutely unconscious. One does not know toward what one moves. One does not know by what one is propelled. The lines of communication between the conscious and the unconscious zones of the human psyche have all been cut, and we have been split in two.[9]

Campbell wrote this in 1949. The unique dilemma for people of his era was that, for the first time, huge numbers were questioning and/or rejecting the old coordinating mythologies, and yet the group culture was not oriented toward supporting a more individual search for meaning. His words spoke prophetically of the cultural revolution of the 1960s and, perhaps even more so, the Me Decade of the 1970s—a time when many people stepped away from conventional career paths, each of them looking for a personal way that was more meaningful. Inherent in this searching was a desire to heal the split between "the conscious and the unconscious zones of the human psyche."

In *Hare Brain, Tortoise Mind,* Guy Claxton highlights this conscious-unconscious split by describing two types of intelligence.[10] "Hare brain" is the fast, logical, goal-oriented thinking that is so highly valued in the modern working world. In contrast, "tortoise mind" is a slower, more meandering state of mind that doesn't seek to solve or fix or change. In its most extreme forms, the goal of a tortoise-mind activity is to have no goal at all. Meditation is an obvious example; others include sitting on a mountaintop, walking on a beach, or daydreaming. Even when a tortoise-mind activity involves a goal, such as gardening, fishing, writing a poem, or painting a picture, often the point of the activity is the state of mind achieved as much as the product produced. However inner stillness can be created, tortoise mind opens a person to the wellspring of the unconscious, allowing inspiration and meaning to come bubbling through. Tortoise mind is the poet awaiting the next line of a poem, the scientist seeking a flash of insight, the artist clearing the mind to be able to see, or the ascetic listening for the word of God. In the mad rush of the modern world—this "hare-brained existence" of ours—tortoise mind is often considered abnormal or, at best, an indulgence we sometimes allow ourselves. But for people who are questioning, rejecting, or trying to deepen the coordinating mythology they have inherited, the call to quiet reflection is neither abnormal nor indulgent. For many, it is lifeblood.

Again, there are many ways to access tortoise mind, a solitary fast in the wilderness being just one. As described earlier, Steven happened upon a rudimentary version of this practice during his travels through the deserts of Nevada and California. Being more a visionary than an English professor, he found in this practice a saner, healthier way to access the tortoise-mind state that was so essential to his being. For a man who had veered so far off course, that practice would give him the direction he so desperately needed. When after one of his early trips Steven declared, "I am a vision quest guide," he claimed this new work as a rudder by which he would set his new course, even if he was only just beginning to imagine the outline of the journey ahead.

If *purpose* in life is to be found in what a person commits to doing—the life course that is being set with a rudder—then *meaning* is the wind that fills those sails, the *inspiration* that drives that person forward. Meaning and inspiration have to be rediscovered over and over, lest the person become stagnant and stuck. For Steven (and Meredith too), the best method for doing that was to spend several days alone in the desert. In time, this became an annual ritual, with each of them doing a four-day desert fast in late winter or early spring. For Steven, writing, teaching, and guiding were the purposeful activities that gave him direction, but it was in the ceremony of a desert fast that he rediscovered the meaning that would propel him forward through the coming year.

The Purpose Circle as Practiced Ritual

If meaning and inspiration are rediscovered over and over, then becoming twice-born may be just the beginning of a long process of becoming more authentically human. The twice-born transformation of which Campbell speaks—from dependent adolescent to autonomous adult—is perhaps the most significant rite of passage in a person's life. And yet most of us will have a number of other important crossings: from single person to life partner; from life partner to parent (or perhaps, from life partner to divorcee); from working adult to community elder. These and other major changes in identity will become more deeply embedded in a person's psyche if they are marked well by a meaningful ceremony. The ritual of the Purpose Circle, as culmination of a four-day wilderness fast, is simply one way to mark such a major life change.

The ceremony of a wilderness fast doesn't require a participant to have any specific cultural orientation or belief system. It is equally appropriate for a religious person whose story draws deeply from an ancestral faith or an atheist who has left behind such beliefs and practices. What matters most is that participants are willing to look at the lifestories they have been telling about themselves, whatever they might be.

For a moment, step inside the world of someone who has been called to do this practice:

A major change in my life has come and I feel a strong urge to mark it well. Time now to renew the story I tell about myself. Turning again into another personal cycle of death-and-rebirth, I commit to doing a wilderness fast. During the months of preparation, I ask myself repeatedly: *What of my old story is dying? And what do I need to carry over to enliven the chapter soon to come?* I ask and I answer. I answer and I ask. *For whom am I living and for what?*

For four days I sit alone, I fast, and I live without walls that would separate me from the natural world. Isolated. Emptied. Exposed. During the first few days of the fast, I hold a Death Lodge where I try to work out some of the relationship issues that are keeping me stuck in the old story. When that is done, I choose a site for the Purpose Circle and then build a circle of stones that represents the new life I am calling in, each stone being chosen to represent an important person or aspect of this life.

At sunset of the chosen evening, either on day three or day four, I step inside the Purpose Circle leaving behind all the preparatory questions and all the people to whom I have said goodbye. The time has come just *to be* my story, to sit in this

Purpose Circle and declare to myself and to the world, "This is who I am." Hour after hour, I offer to the night sky my uncertainties and my prayers, my songs and my laments. With the crescent moon serving as midwife, the world around me contracts, pushing me slowly through the birth canal. When the first ray of sunlight hits, I am reborn. I *am* my new story.[11]

By stepping back into the ritual of a Purpose Circle, year after year, Steven turned his life into an upward spiral of "becoming." With each yearly fast, he would remake his lifestory and then spend the following year living out that new story. By the next year, though, the story would again need to be renewed. Each death and rebirth represented a quantum leap, another turn upward into more fully becoming "Steven Foster." This was Steven's greatest achievement in life. After inheriting a religious worldview that left him ill-prepared for his adult life, he managed to find a spiritual practice that worked for him. This practice, which has roots in most of the major religions, including the Christian faith he had been given, allowed him to continually rediscover his own authentic storyline.

Just as the Death Lodge helped Steven to keep his relationships current, the practice of the Purpose Circle kept the vision of his life current. If one day he died suddenly, he would go to his grave with ideas for books, programs, and teachings that had never been realized. But even if his life was never going to be *complete,* when his end did finally come, Steven would certainly be *current*. He would die knowing he had lived his final days following his own vision.

The Denial of Death

"This is one aspect of the basic human predicament," the psychologist Abraham Maslow has written, "that we are simultaneously worms and gods."[12] Like worms, we eat and we shit, we get sick and we die. Like gods, we are blessed with the capacity to dream and reflect, to imagine and be inspired, to create and be fulfilled. In Maslow's words, this godlike quality is our capacity to "actualize potential," to enjoy "full humanness."[13] Or in Campbell's words, this is our capacity to become twice-born: to die to the group mythology that we have inherited, so that we might be reborn in a more authentic way.

In the world of the god-worm, not all is glorious and expansive. Our godlike capacity to reflect demands that we each grapple with the agonizing truth of this wormlike existence: One day I will die and then decay. For most animals, the experience of death is usually played out in a relative flash. A few minutes of fear, anguish and pain and then it's over. In contrast, the human animal, beginning as early as age four or five, is able to anticipate its own demise. As a god-worm, we each have the capacity to dream and reflect, but we also have the capacity to be anxious and afraid, to be terrified and trembling. We may be blessed to be gods, but we are also cursed.

In his groundbreaking book, *The Denial of Death*, Ernest Becker pays homage to the work of Sigmund Freud, acknowledging his great discovery: that the cause of psychological illness is often a fear of self—of one's emotions, impulses, memories, and potentialities.[14] But rather than the repression of sexuality, as Freud has argued, Becker suggests that the primary repression for the human animal is the denial of death. Our deepest need, Becker argues, is to deny our fundamental anxiety about death and annihilation; and yet, "it is life itself which awakens it, and so we must shrink from being fully alive."[15] Each of the great coordinating mythologies that has been handed down for millennia has offered its own resolution to this great existential problem. And so it can't be emphasized enough that to become twice-born—to step outside an inherited tradition and ask alone big questions about death and the afterlife—can leave a person vulnerable and exposed. In Becker's words:

> . . . to see the world as it really is is devastating and terrifying. It achieves the very result that the child has painfully built his character over the years in order to avoid: it *makes routine, automatic, secure, self-confident activity impossible.* It makes thoughtless living in the world of men an impossibility. It places a trembling animal at the mercy of the entire cosmos and the problem of the meaning of it.[16]

And yet this is the very goal of the wilderness fast. Place a human animal alone in the desert, denying it all social distractions. Deprive it of food so it might viscerally know what it means to be dying. And expose that animal to the great expanse of the night sky, "the entire cosmos and the problem of the meaning of it." Like a worm, isolated, emptied, exposed. Like a god, free to create ritual, to offer prayers, to ask the great questions of purpose and meaning. That juxtaposition creates a tortoise-mind practice that is uniquely powerful, which is why versions of it can be found at the roots of most major religions.

The wilderness fast is uniquely powerful and yet, for some, it is also very risky. If qualified guides are supporting a wilderness fast, the physical risk is minimal; a person is far more likely to be harmed during a typical week in the city than during a fast in the desert. The risk of the wilderness fast is much more psychological and existential. *Am I prepared to be plucked out of the comfort zone of group culture and placed starkly alone in the desert wilderness? Am I willing, for four days and nights, to examine my own personal myth, the story that ultimately I must carry to my own grave?*

The risk of the wilderness fast is considerable, but so, too, is its boon. Returning to Steven in the desert, this time in 1980, we visit him during one of his most important fasts:

> It dawns on me that no longer am I seeking answers. I'm seeking ways, means to ends. Having asked questions about life meaning and purpose until I was blue, blue, blue, not knowing, I stopped all that nonsense and not too long ago began to go about seeking ways to accomplish my purposes.
>
> I am not one who can talk to the wind. Rather, I am one who the wind chooses to fill and send forth with intent. I am the wind's answer to my own questions about purpose and destiny.
>
> Having passed the mid-point of life, I am now exhaling the long inwardly drawn breath that brought me to midlife, sighing away each year till my death. I am very fortunate to have lived so long, with so many lives, loves, adventures, children, places seen, catastrophes endured. Surely life has been good to me.[17]

Here we see Steven discovering that, after so many years of doing the hard work of building a Purpose Circle, his inner circle of identity, meaning, and purpose was now basically complete. As he said, "surely life has been good to him." But what he couldn't know was that, at the age of forty-one, his life was well past its "mid-point." Rather than four more decades to go, he only had two.

Mortality Made Real

For the average person living in the fast-paced world of the city, a wilderness fast is a uniquely powerful way to practice the ancient art of *momento mori:* remembering that I will die, so that I might live more fully. "[Momento mori] isn't primarily a practice of thinking of one's last hour, or of death as a physical phenomenon," the monk David Steindl-Rast has written, "it is a seeing of every moment of life against the horizon of death, and a challenge to incorporate that awareness of dying into every moment so as to become more fully alive."[18] Leaving behind the routines, defenses, and distractions of day-to-day living and sitting alone in the desert for four days allows a person to gaze across the land of life, out toward the horizon of death.

Keeping death directly in view, whether in a monastery or on a desert fast, can be a powerful practice, and yet, it is still only a symbolic exercise in dying. No spiritual practice asks a person to take on questions about meaning and purpose quite like an actual brush with death. Imagine again that you have a life-threatening illness and you are told you have only weeks, months, or a few years left to live. With a power and immediacy unlike that of any spiritual exercise, you will be forced to look toward that fast-approaching horizon. Or perhaps instead you have a brush with death that is more sudden: a heart attack, a car accident, a violent assault. In an instant, that thin veneer of psychological defense—Becker's denial of death—will be stripped away, leaving you to stare directly at death's door. Whether the threat of death comes gradually or suddenly, it will likely raise some of life's biggest questions. Some might say: *Why me? Why now?* Others might ask instead: *Have I done enough with my life? What shall I do with the time remaining?*

What separated Steven from most other mortals is that reflecting about his own death was already a conscious practice, even before he became ill. For years he had focused on the small deaths, repeatedly looking for what was sick and dying in his life that he might let it go. When his breathing started to become more difficult, death ceased to be a mental concept, an abstraction meant to focus and inspire. Death instead became a frequent companion, especially late at night when he awakened short of breath.

The first signs of Steven's illness appeared nearly two decades before he died. From that point on, the constant progression of his breathlessness demanded that he stare out at a horizon that was fast-approaching. Steven often flinched, he often despaired, but seldom did he avert his eyes. Death became a given, both the inevitable outcome and the ultimate measure of his life. This was yet another version of the Purpose Circle, but rather than a yearly event, this became his near-daily practice. Here was a ritual that did not require solitude, fasting, or exposure. With every sputtering cough, every gasping breath, Steven could feel himself lurching toward the horizon's edge.

Death as the Final Giveaway

The literature of the world is replete with stories of young women and men learning to "grow up," people spiraling upward into fuller versions of themselves. By comparison, precious little is written about how to "grow down" (and most of that coming only in the last few decades). If "growing up" means leaving behind the physical dependency of childhood and slowly emerging as an autonomous adult, then "growing down," at least in the physical realm, is just the opposite. Whether it takes years, months, weeks or days, the inexorable decline of disease and old age often robs people of their hard-earned autonomy, causing them to spiral down into the physical dependency of a second childhood.

Despite the physical decline of these last days, many people continue to grow emotionally and spiritually, sometimes at an accelerated rate. For some, this growth may be inspired by a decline that alters the search for purpose and meaning. If the charge of the healthy adult is to produce and to achieve, to love and to give, then the task of the dying person is much the opposite: to release and to surrender, to be loved and to receive the care of others. For some, this is not a simple reversal to make. It begs a question that may be difficult to ask and to answer. *Am I worthy of the love and care that I now so clearly need?*

As with any of us, the beginning of Steven's own answer can be found in his first childhood. He had been raised in a family where the love that was offered was conditional. "You are worthy of love," he had been told, "only if you are a good Christian boy. And to be a good

Christian boy means this . . . and this . . . and this." In 1984, the very year his breathing troubles first began, that early legacy was still with him:

> Perhaps the greatest monster of my life is "lack of faith" that I am truly loved, i.e., loved for myself, for whom and what I am. It may be that I destroy my life, love, and all I hold dear because of this doubt. Because I find it so difficult to believe I am lovable, acceptable, and respectable, I may never attain harmony and balance with my spirit in this life. I say this calmly, rationally, and without heavy self-accusation. It is a <u>fact</u> of my existence— my "karma" as it were. The mountain of my later life that I must climb or suffer the abysmal consequences.[19]

The heart and soul of rites-of-passage work, like hospice caregiving, is supporting people in the midst of their major life transformations. During thirty years of listening to and holding other people's stories, Steven and Meredith offered their own unique gift of love to thousands. Was all that enough to make the little boy in Steven feel lovable in return? Apparently not. Instead, the angst of that little boy continued to serve as major fuel, driving him to write and to teach and to guide. "I may not be lovable," he might have said, "but dammit, I can sure love others and help them to love themselves."

In the later years of his decline, Steven struggled mightily with whether he deserved to be loved, especially when that became coupled with his worsening physical dependency. "Steven always carried angst," Meredith wrote soon after his death, "a struggle with his changes, his unhappiness, his self-doubts. It drove him, and I suppose it drove him these last years, too. At the end the changes just seemed to happen on all levels. They began to eat away at his ability to be creative, and feel like a MAN. And these, as you can imagine, were the hardest of all."[20] Like it or not, the flow of love—who is taking care of whom— was being reversed in Steven's life. Given his upbringing, a second childhood was not what he wanted. Suicide, it often seemed to him, was the only option.

And yet, Steven knew the power of transformation that can be found in the Purpose Circle. Every cell in his body *knew* that power. Whether the ceremony was held at the end of a yearly fast or on a daily basis during his final years, the Purpose Circle was a place where he could restore his own sense of dignity and worth, even as his body was disintegrating. *What do I have to live for? How can I continue to serve this world? What will be my giveaway?* Living those questions on a daily basis forced him to confront the biggest monsters of his life: suffocation terror, an uncertain legacy, and being unworthy of his own love. Coming face to face with these monsters, he was finally able to accept them as part of the man he was and part of the man he would always be.

In the end, suicide was not a viable option for Steven. As his body failed him, he did learn to receive the care he needed. He did come to believe that he was loved and lovable. Rather than stealing life away suddenly, with pills or with a gun, he was able to give himself over to his dying. As he says in his last published book:

> If I must bow before the throne of Lord Death, give me one last chance to show who I really am!
>
> Suicide is a justifiable alternative. But a more satisfying one is to finish the picture, at least until the paint runs out. Only then can we ask for help from the angels and pass through the throne room of death to join the spinners who spin and spin forever.[21]

One final bow before the throne of Death would be Steven's last giveaway. He would offer this to Death, his great teacher, as well as all the people that he, in turn, had taught. But more importantly he would give this gift to Meredith, to his children, and to himself. He was determined to leave the world declaring one last time, "This is who I am!"

Third Home Visit

April 15: Dear doc, thanks for sending me your book. Just finished it and as you said, "it is what it is." And what it is is deeply moving, fascinating, haunting, dark as lightning, soft and hard, dream and metaphor, human and sacred, revelatory and hidden, straightforward and slippery, true and truthful. I wonder if it is just the first of a series. How "literary" is it? Who gives a shit. Just read it for what it is. More to say in person, much more.[1]

April 26: Doc dearest, I need to see you as soon as convenient for you. My meet-and-greet with the new doctor isn't until next week—don't think it'll wait.

The last two mornings I've awakened with bizarre feelings about dying. That is, feeling so rotten (psychotic, schizzy, crazy sick) that I would really rather be done with it all. I wonder if I have reached some kind of toxicity due to the mixing of drugs. By early afternoon, the bodily sensations have let up somewhat. Nights tend to be a kind of hell. I'm at a loss to understand symptoms, considering my psychological appetite to work out and strengthen my body at the gym, my love for my woman, my kids, you, and a new project, a screen play called "The Drunken Bus."

Why can't you be my "primary doc"? I won't give you up. I won't. I won't![2]

– Steven Foster, emails to the author

Third Home Visit

Thursday, May 1

A half-mile short of Steven and Meredith's home, I parked my car at a trailhead leading steeply up the side of Mount Tamalpais. Fog was dripping off the pine trees, making the ground damp but not slippery. I let Liza off leash a short distance from the road. A foxhound, tall and lean with an hourglass body, she dashed ahead, her long legs barely keeping pace with her fast-sniffing nose. I followed behind, not sure what scent we were after or what route we'd be taking. *Doesn't really matter,* I told myself, *not nearly enough time to get to the mountaintop.* When last I had spoken to Meredith, she had said to come after ten o'clock. That gave us ninety minutes: half of it to get our hearts pounding on the way up, the other half to get us back down.

The huff and puff of climbing became a steady focus, turning the walk into a morning meditation. For me, this was both Death Lodge and Purpose Circle, an opportunity to get current with the people and the problems that were jumbling around inside. I churned through recent details from my life: an article I was writing, dinner the night before with a friend, yesterday's clinic, a sick fellow in the hospital. After a half-hour, though, I was empty. No great worries. No major regrets.

Eventually the trail leveled out, taking me beyond the forest and out to the Mountain Home Inn and its promise of a panoramic view. I was greeted instead by a stream of fog pouring down the mountain. A check of the time told me I had only minutes to linger anyway, so I stopped long enough to consider what was waiting down below. No clue. For the first time, though, I had little concern about what was to come with Steven. *Just show up. I am who I am. I know what I need to know.*

The descent was equally void of anxiety or anticipation. Arriving at the car, I made the two-minute drive to the home of the Littles, re-parked at the top of the driveway, and left Liza in the back seat. *A tired dog is a good dog,* I told myself. She had gone twice as far as I had and four times as fast. *She should be one tired dog.*

I bypassed the main house and headed directly to Steven and Meredith's rooms. Again, Meredith greeted me at the door. Behind her I could hear the loud lament of a song by Beck, which I recognized. After breaking up with a girlfriend of many years, he had recorded *Sea Change,* a collection of hauntingly beautiful songs. "It's only you that I'm losing," Beck was now wailing, "guess I'm doing fine."

"This is such a gorgeous album," I said.

"Gorgeous and sad," Meredith answered. "The only music appropriate for a morning like this. Steven had another hard night. I was trying to give us both something to focus on."

"A hard night in what way?"

"Come in and speak to him." She motioned me to follow. "He'll tell you."

Inside the main room, Steven was sitting on the side of the bed, looking bedraggled. His hair was tied back, but still out of place, and his T-shirt and sweatpants looked as if he had slept in them. Even if he had forever played the part of the mountain man, he usually had been well groomed. Today he didn't seem to care.

"Hey doc, you made it." He got up slowly, arms wide open, waiting for me to come to him for a welcoming hug. Close up, I smelled something fetid. *Probably a bad case of morning breath.*

Meredith turned off the music, leaving us with the swooshing rise and collapsing fall of the oxygen machine.

The doctor in me did a quick assessment. *He looks tired, but his breathing isn't labored. Not hot or sweaty, so a fever's not likely. Maybe this is just lack of sleep.*

"So where's your dog?" said Steven, recalling my email from the day before. "Thought the two of you were going for a romp in the woods."

"The romping has been done and she's back in the car recovering." Bad as he looked, I decided to keep the banter to a minimum. "So Meredith tells me you had a bad night."

"Bad week is more like it, doc."

Doc it is, I told myself. "All of me" may have shown up today, but given the way he looked, it was the doctor who would take the lead. *Set aside the friendly banter. Set aside the planning of the hospice fast.*

I grabbed a chair, put it directly in front of him and sat down. On the floor between us was a nearly-empty bottle of whiskey.

"So tell me about the week, Steven."

"Hmmm," he sighed softly. "No, not that. Not yet. I'd rather talk about your book. That's more important than what this ol' carcass has been through."

"I beg to differ," I said, suppressing a powerful urge to hear what he might say about my writing. "Look, we can talk about the book another time. Today it's your health we need to focus on."

"But doc, what you've written *is* important. It'll be part of your legacy someday, nothing less. Just like my books are for me." He picked up one of his wrists with the thumb and finger of the other hand, raised it up in the air and let it drop. "This body will soon be dead, but not those books. They're as close to forever as you and I are gonna get."

As he spoke, I watched his breathing more closely. He was talking in full sentences, but every once in a while he would give extra attention to an inhalation, leaning forward with his hands on his knees and using pursed lips to suck in the air.

Meredith came over to him, placing her hand on his shoulder. "Yesterday he put the finishing touches on his latest book and sent it off for the final layout. Should go to the printer in a few weeks."

"Yeah," said Steven frowning, "a book I had to finish in thirty-minute stretches. Pecked out with one finger, one letter at a time."

"Ah, but it's finished," I said. "One more piece of eternity, done. And I, for one, can't wait to read it." I placed my hand on his knee and shook it gently. "But Steven, I'm still stuck on this body of yours. However impermanent it may be, we need to get it back on track. Get you back to writing. Back to creating more of a legacy. Today, our main job is to play doctor-patient."

He relented, finally speaking about the troubles of the past week. Some of it was old and familiar: waking up at night short of breath, desperately needing a breathing treatment. Instead of falling back asleep, though, now he was staying awake for hours.

"The longer I'm awake, the more this room turns into a haunted house. A carnival ride straight through hell. I'll be staring out at the trees and suddenly they morph into monsters or gargoyles. Or I try to distract myself with television, only to have people be suddenly decapitated, bloody heads rolling off to the side. That then gets me thinking about my own dying. The scenes of that are just as ugly."

"Sounds terrible."

"Yeah, doc. Feels like I'm scaling a wall. A wall of pain that separates me from death." His eyes were now on the ground, as if he didn't want to see the imaginary barrier he was describing. "But now there's no light to show me the way over the wall. Nothing but demons and dark shadows."

I asked several more questions about what he was seeing, hearing, and thinking. *He's lucid,* I decided. *Able to know what's real and what's not.* Still, the visions were terrifying him.

"I remember what you said last visit, Steven. One day, home may be like heaven. The next day, hell. Same place, but the world offers back a different reflection."

"Damn right, and now it's hell of the worst kind."

"But you've never been one to live life halfway, have you?" I said this as a genuine compliment, recognizing the heroic in Steven.

He refused my words instantly, waving his hands back and forth. "All I want is to do this halfway!" His face had changed. No longer an older man, he had turned into a frightened little boy. "Doc," he pleaded, "you gotta help me."

"Right, Steven." I put my hand back on his knee. "That's why I'm here. Let's see if we can figure this out."

The time had come to play traditional doctor: ask about symptoms, examine for physical signs, recognize patterns of disease, and consider tests to confirm or deny my suspicions. Our previous "difficult conversations" had defined the way forward, at least as far as options to be considered. No ERs, no hospitals, no medical miracles. I needed to focus on what could be done for him here in his own bedroom, at least until he got to meet his new doctor.

"So tell me about your cold and how it's affected your breathing."

Near the top of the list of possible causes for delirium is oxygen deprivation. But to my surprise, his respiratory symptoms weren't that bad. A runny nose with some sinus congestion. Some coughing, but not that much phlegm. No fevers. Breathing troubles no worse than usual. Most importantly, his oxygen saturation levels hadn't fallen.

Meredith put the oximeter clip on his finger to check the oxygen level again. "87%," she said. "Pretty good for him."

I listened closely to his lungs. They sounded the same as before: distant breath sounds, almost inaudible, but no noises suggesting pneumonia or heart failure. After finishing a fuller exam, I gave them a summary of what I heard and saw, focusing especially on the risk of lung infection.

"I don't think it's the cold that's been messin' with me," Steven replied. "More likely a bad mix of medicines. I've been tied to these drugs for so long, tied with chemical strands refined in some lab. I think those strands may be going haywire now, getting all crisscrossed."

Meredith gave me a current list of his medicines that began with all those for breathing: low-dose steroids and a collection of inhalers. All of them, especially the steroids, could contribute to anxiety, agitation, and, in extreme cases, hallucinations. None of these were new, though, and their doses hadn't been changed for months.

"They've always made me feel like a cowboy on a bucking bronco," said Steven, "but this week the ride hasn't been any worse than usual."

Next were psychoactive drugs capable of causing hallucinations. Morphine was the biggest concern, but he told me he was using it judiciously during the day, and not at all during the middle-of-the-night episodes.

His two anxiety meds, Klonopin and Xanax, and his antidepressant, Zoloft, were also possibilities, but again their doses hadn't been changed in months.

The only recent change, he admitted, was his whiskey. In an effort to finish his book, he had started drinking again. The ups and downs of intoxication, however mild, could certainly be part of this picture.

"Whiskey is my best friend and my worst enemy," said Steven. "It gives me energy to write, even if only for thirty minutes at a pop."

Another potential culprit was insomnia. A classic trio of symptoms at the end of life is pain-depression-insomnia, with each one capable of worsening the other two. I wondered whether breathlessness-anxiety-insomnia might be creating a similar vicious cycle for Steven. In the past, a single dose of an anxiety medicine might have sorted this out, but not anymore.

"Lots of factors here," I offered in summary. "You wake up with a low oxygen level, so that makes you prone to confusion. Chronic lack of sleep probably makes that worse. Then if Xanax doesn't put you back to sleep, it can actually contribute to the confusion. On top of that, you might be having some alcohol withdrawal after not drinking for many hours."

I paused to let that sink in. Steven wasn't his usual animated self, but still he seemed to be taking in what I said.

"All that stuff is physical, Steven, and all of it we can work on. And we will. But before I leap to prescribing even more drugs, I want to go deeper. I want to go below the chemical surface, to the actual source of your nightmares."

I described briefly a talk I had been giving for years about the psychological progression of serious illness. The middle portions of the Kübler-Ross stages—anger, bargaining, and depression—often become a merry-go-round of grief and loss. Around the whirling reds of anger, the spiraling blacks of depression, the bargaining mind desperately tries to grab hold of any kind of central pole that will steady it. Anger, bargaining, and depression cease to be stages you walk through, one after the other. Instead they become a dizzying spin that just won't stop.

"I call it cycling," said Meredith. "Constant cycling." She described the first big grieving that came when Steven had to start using oxygen for any kind of exercise. "You say to yourself, 'Okay I've finally accepted that one.' But then it changes, and you realize you have to do that accepting all over again." She offered the full litany of Steven's major losses. No more wilderness trips at high altitude. Difficulty having sex. Using oxygen even just to sleep. Not being able to do simple chores around the house. And finally, having to leave his home in order to get to sea level. "Constant cycling. One loss after another. It never stops."

While Meredith talked, I watched Steven as much as her. The

weight of what she said seemed to press down on him, his shoulders drooping forward, his face sagging. Soon the little boy had returned. *About eight years old,* I guessed.

"So the hallucinations may be new," I said, "but you've been climbing this wall of grief for a long time, haven't you?"

Tears began to fall silently down his schoolboy cheeks.

I placed a hand back on his knee, using the other to shift my chair as close to him as I could.

The tears became an audible sob.

Pulling him toward me, I wrapped my arms around him. Hidden inside his loose-fitting T-shirt was a boniness that surprised me. I held on tightly, as if the embrace was all that was holding his body together. I was no longer doctor, student, or friend, or even brother. I was father to a very young Steven. If only for a minute, I was holding a frightened, little boy. I held him long enough for the man to slowly reemerge, for Steven to reclaim his full physical form.

When his tears stopped, I let him go and pulled my chair back even farther than before. "Those monsters you've been seeing, Steven, you've been carrying those inside you for a long time. Haven't you?"

"Yeah, doc." He blew his nose, a loud honking noise. "So what do you got in your bag of tricks to get rid of 'em?"

"For the grief and loss that's inflating those monsters? Not much. But there is something that might help, might make you feel less alone in your struggle. I'd like to get hospice out here, and soon. If only to give you access to nursing visits in the middle of the night, the next time a crisis hits."

Meredith's eyes widened some, her body shifting forward, her head nodding up and down. This was help she obviously would welcome.

I explained what the fullest version of hospice might look like: regular visits from nurses, a social worker, the chaplain, home health aides, maybe a volunteer. After some discussion, Steven made it clear that all he wanted for now was the crisis support. Later, maybe more.

"Then it'll be the bare minimum," I said. "A nurse visiting once a week, nurses available for any crisis, and a social worker checking in by phone every couple of weeks."

"What about the appointment with the new doctor?" asked Meredith.

"Good question." I paused to think.

Bringing hospice on board would change everything. All of Steven's care would be at home, with nurses available for urgent needs. And even though I was an hour away, I was more committed to making home visits than most doctors, even one whose office was only ten minutes away. This was no longer about roles or boundaries or borders. *Just show up,* I told myself. *Show up and do what needs to be done.*

"It's up to you two. You can go see the new doc, or you can cancel the visit and have me as the primary. Whichever you prefer. With hospice able to come out for a crisis, the long drive from my home is far less of an issue."

"You mean you can be my primary doc?" asked Steven.

I nodded yes.

"Well that's a relief." He smiled for the first time that day. "If I'd only known that, I would have asked for hospice months ago."

"No, Steven. I don't think you were ready back then. As it is, you've had impeccable nursing from Meredith all this time. And I've filled in with a mix of friend and hospice physician."

"And wilderness guide, too," said Steven.

"Fair enough. But today, mostly doctor."

I returned again to his physical well-being, suggesting a few possible adjustments in medications. No change in the longer-acting Klonopin, but use less of the Xanax. After the early morning awakenings, try morphine in small doses. Consider using Thorazine at night, both for sleep and to treat the hallucinations.

After some discussion, Steven agreed to the new plan. I borrowed their phone, first calling in the new medicine to a pharmacy and then arranging an admission with the local hospice. Their intake nurse promised a visit the following week.

"One last piece of the plan." I looked directly at Steven. "As important as hospice and the new meds may be, you gotta go easy on the whiskey."

We talked more about how much he was drinking and how best to wean himself.

"Yeah," he said, "I've been using the whiskey to feed my muse. Maybe now, with the book done, I can let it go."

"So with that book finished, what comes next?" I was looking for anything that might inspire him, but his eyes seemed blank. Staring lifelessly ahead might be normal for someone else, but for Steven, a man bigger than life itself, it was a terrible sign.

Finally, he did his best to answer, rambling a little about two projects: *The Drunken Bus* screenplay and an autobiography he had started years before. Even then, his words soon faded.

"Sounds like you're still searching for what's next?"

"Yeah, suppose you're right."

Suddenly I was struck by the Catch-22 of Steven's life. He needed to write to have a reason to live and he needed whiskey to be able to write. But he needed to quit the whiskey to keep the internal monsters away. He was trapped.

"Brings me back to our first visit, Steven. Back to one of the very first questions I ever asked you. What do you have to live for?"

He gave his familiar moan again, looking down at the floor. "Besides writing, I suppose there's the teaching. Maybe this hospice fast we've been talkin' about, maybe that'll happen. Then M and I are supposed to help Gigi and Win do the month-long training. And that's only weeks away." He sighed, as if the air released was just more vital energy being lost.

"Scott, I've wanted to ask you about the month-long," said Meredith. "Do you think the trip back to Big Pine is safe for Steven?"

I answered them straight. Even if Steven got over his cold, even if we got the mix of drugs sorted, he would still be weak. A trip to 4,000 feet would be a risk.

"But if Steven can't go back to the mountain," I suggested, "why not bring the mountain to him? You could hold the month-long training in that cathedral of trees right outside your bedroom door. Meetings here in the morning. Send people out to Mount Tam in the afternoon. Back here in the evening for stories."

A light went on in Steven's eyes. *Maybe, just maybe,* he seemed to be thinking.

"Oh, but do I really have another training in me?" he said,

grimacing. "Not to mention another book."

He looked over to Meredith, realizing what he had just said. She matched his look without a flinch. Whatever you want, she seemed to reply.

"So who am I if I can't teach? Who am I if I can't write? Maybe it's time to pack up the ol' smudge bowl. Put the computer away, too." He paused to get his breath, drawing oxygen in through pursed lips. "Time for me to find a barren spot alone on the mountain and build me a circle of stones."

"Your final Purpose Circle?"

"That's right. The final stand."

"Not sure when that time will come, Steven, but I have to ask: Are you ready?"

"Damn right, I am. My legacy's done. I've given them all I've got. Ain't no more down in the well."

"And quite a legacy it is, Steven. You've touched thousands and thousands of people. Changed lots of lives in a very big way."

"Yeah, I suppose you're right," he said, deflecting the compliment. "But it's my children I worry about." He coughed a few times and then had to wait awhile to catch his breath. "Did I do right by them? I can't help wonder. That's the hard question, the most important question."

He talked some about his regrets. What he had done, what he hadn't done. As he spoke, I noticed the pauses to catch his breath were getting longer, more frequent.

"Maybe I'll get better. Maybe I'll have more to write, more to teach. Maybe not. Who knows? Maybe all I have left to give them is my death."

"How you die can be a gift, Steven. That final memory of your last days will mean a lot to your family. I know. I've seen it over and over."

"And you, doc. You said you'd be there, right?"

I pulled a small black velvet bag from my shirt pocket and, out of that, plucked the pfennig he had given me. "Steven, your account is already paid in full. The boatman is at your service."

He grinned, placing his hand over his heart.

I stood up and placed my hand on top of his. With help from me, he also stood and we hugged. I stepped back, releasing him to his seat on the bed.

"Look, Steven, I gotta go. Not because I have anywhere better to be, but because you're running out of gas."

He offered a weak protest, which I rebuffed.

"But before you go," he said, "don't we get to meet Liza, the wonder dog?"

I glanced over at Meredith, who nodded her head. "Sure, but just for a minute. And then I'm outta here."

I went to the car and brought Liza back, releasing her once we were inside. Surrounded by so many unfamiliar smells, she worked herself into a sniffing frenzy, more interested in the nooks and crannies of the room than the two people who were trying to say hello. Her exuberance was a startling counterpoint to Steven's waning energy, causing me to worry that she might be too much for him. Steven, though, was obviously entertained. *Give them some room,* I chided myself. *Each to their own pleasures.*

"Okay, Liza," I finally said. "That's enough. Time for us to go. Time for this man to get some rest."

"Hey, doc, I'll release you two, but only if you make me a promise."

I braced myself.

"Next time I want more real conversation. Not just about my health, but about your book. About your book and mine."

"If you've got the energy, Steven, then I've got the time."

We smiled in agreement. Another hug with Steven, a softer embrace with Meredith, and Liza and I were gone.

Part 4

The Great Ballcourt

The first thing you will recognize is the landscape. The Great Ballcourt seems no different than the world you left behind. Could it be a mirror-image? You must look on this seemingly identical world without illusions. The Lords of Death are everywhere and in everything. You are in the Underworld and all around you is a great circle of witnesses. You are dancing with Death on the Great Ballcourt.

. . . It is quite possible to see the Great Ballcourt as fulfillment, not failure or catastrophe. Every day you have practiced your dance on one of the ballcourts of your life. You have danced with the "monsters" of your karma—your loved ones, your people, your work, the things and cares of your life. As you grew, you learned to dance. You began to see that your dance with karma contained the same movements as the dance with Death on the Great Ballcourt.[1]

– Steven Foster, *The Great Ballcourt Vision Fast*

The Great Ballcourt

The Body as the Ballcourt

Imagine that your life is nearing its end. The time has come to prepare for your final crossing. Long ago you stepped onto Decision Road, slowly learning to surrender to the little deaths that life has asked of you. That road brought you to the Death Lodge, a place where you learned lessons about how to keep current your most important relationships. Beyond that came the work of the Purpose Circle, where you gave your life meaning through the intertwining of deep reflection and purposeful activity. Now, a life well lived soon will end. One last time you visit the Death Lodge to say your goodbyes. One last time you step into the Purpose Circle to accept and to embody all that you've been and all that you are. And now, the summons arrives. The time has come to step onto the Great Ballcourt of your dying.

This final dance with death does not take place in some imaginary otherworld. It is real and it is now. You have arrived on the Great Ballcourt, which is your own physical body. This is the great container that will hold the drama of your last dance with death. Family and friends gather around you as spectators, but much of this dance is inside you, invisible to their eyes. Some of these witnesses stand in awe of what they are able to see. Others shudder and look away. They all know that, someday, they must also step onto their own ballcourt.

Your arrival on the Great Ballcourt is well expressed by words from medieval Europe: *Mors certa, hora incerta.*[2] *Death is certain, its hour uncertain.* Perhaps your arrival on the Ballcourt will be sudden, your life cut short by accident, violence, or anatomical failure. More likely, your dying will stretch out over hours to days, maybe even weeks to months. If it does, and if you are willing to face up to what is happening, your end may be foreseeable, even if its exact hour remains uncertain.

The physical conditions of your ballcourt, your own dying body, are also impossible to predict. Some features of this final decline, though, are common. When the body first begins to weaken, strenuous activities like hiking, swimming, or playing tennis have to be stopped. As the force of life continues to seep away, even simple walking becomes difficult. Eventually, an ever-weakening body must be confined to a wheelchair, then later a house, and finally a single bed. As the body slows, hare-brained thinking will also have to give way to a tortoise-minded existence. Each day a dying person must rediscover how to be a participant in an ever-shrinking world. The question may often arise: *How do I call forth what little vitality I have left to be with the people I love and to take pleasure in what is to come?*

At some point in this decline, a dying person's appetite starts to fade, leaving only an occasional craving for comfort foods, and later not even that. With energy limited, the body shunts glucose, its most efficient source of fuel, away from the muscles and toward the brain, wanting the mind to remain clear. If nutrition is lacking for too long, however, even the brain will eventually be forced to run on ketones instead of glucose. Acting much like a natural painkiller, ketones slow thinking and may even cause a mild euphoria. Thirst for liquids may also fade, causing progressive dehydration, which further clouds the mind.[3]

Depending on the underlying illness and the treatments a dying person does (or doesn't) receive, this common pathway of decline can be further complicated by physical symptoms. Pain or nausea may cause greater or lesser discomfort. Shortness of breath may make it seem as if death will happen any minute. Emotional troubles, combined with neurological irritation, may cause anxiety, agitation, or restlessness. Incontinence of bowel and bladder, along with skin breakdown, can make a person dependent on others for the most intimate care, raising issues of privacy, dignity, and pride. Near the very end, respiratory muscles may become so weak that the dying person can't clear any phlegm, making for a loud, moist breathing that upsets loved ones who are nearby.

Whatever conditions you encounter on the ballcourt of your own body, these physical challenges are likely to seem capricious and, at times, beyond your control. In the absence of good end-of-life care, these symptoms can cause great suffering, but with the help of a hospice or palliative care team, most of them can be ameliorated.[4]

Barring a sudden, unexpected death, you have the opportunity to make a few important choices that may impact what happens at the end of your life.

Where do I want to spend my last days? At home, in a hospital, or in a nursing facility?

What kind of care do I want pursued on my behalf? A battle for life at all costs, a surrendering into death, or something in-between?

Who are the medical allies I want to call in? A team of doctors and nurses dedicated to aggressive care, or a more varied group of caregivers, including some well versed in hospice and palliative medicine?

To answer these questions, you must be prepared to have a series of "difficult conversations": first with yourself, then with loved ones, and finally with your doctors. Having done that, you can then write your wishes down as "advance directives."* This is your chance to tell the world how it is you envision your final dance on the Great Ballcourt.

The Dance Inside

Underlying illness, lack of food or water, and medication effects may leave a dying person disoriented and confused, unable to engage with those who visit. More and more, the person may drift away into a private reality. What is happening inside, though, is not merely a clouded confusion caused by physical changes. On the ballcourt of the body, the dying person is alone, doing a final dance with death. This may be a dance of severance, a dance at the threshold, a dance of incorporation, or some of all three. Severance: *What am I leaving behind?* Threshold: *What essential part of me is being revealed during this crossing?* Incorporation: *What is my vision of what lies beyond?*

Two experienced hospice nurses, Maggie Callanan and Patricia Kelley, wrote *Final Gifts,* a book that describes the inner processing and communication that may happen during this final stage of dying.[5] If the decline stretches over days to weeks, a dying person may shift back and forth between the social world of wrapping up a life and the inner world of preparing for a final exit. This inner world is a dreamlike

* See Resources, page 169 for more information about advance directives.

state where thinking is comprised of preverbal images and allegories rather than linear ideas and abstractions. Callanan and Kelley call this inner state "nearing death awareness." They contrast it with more widely published accounts of the "near-death experience" in which a person faces the sudden threat of death, journeys briefly out of the body or toward a light, only to be jerked back to life.[6,7] Though these dramatic stories may be more riveting, only about one-tenth of deaths are sudden. A slower dying, with its nearing death awareness, is the more common version of the final crossing.

Given the dreamlike quality of nearing death awareness, the dying person may often use language that is highly symbolic, unexpected, or obscure. Because this language can be difficult to follow, the person may be labeled as "out of it," "confused," "hallucinating," or "dreaming." Even worse, caregivers may become frustrated, annoyed, or condescending, perhaps even administering a sedative to treat this supposed problem. Any of these responses may prevent the people who are keeping vigil from receiving the dying person's "final gifts."

The dying of Aldie Hine is a moving example of one man's nearing death awareness. Aldie was fortunate to be surrounded by people who were open enough to receive his final gifts. These gifts were so profound that they would influence Steven and Meredith for years to come, both in exploring the symbolic death of a rite of passage and, much later, in preparing for Steven's physical death. In *Last Letter to the Pebble People*, Aldie's nearing death awareness first becomes obvious days before his death:

> [Aldie] was engaged in an exchange that seemed to have the urgency of decision about it. He was still able to amuse us briefly with a whimsy or an unexpected joke, but for the most part he was *working*. There is just no other word for it. Working at something, resolving something—all through a dialogue with someone or something we could not see.
>
> Early that first evening, Joey [a son-in-law] had asked him if there were someone in the room with them and Aldie had nodded.
>
> "Who is it?" Joey asked.
>
> "Death," Aldie answered.

"What is death like?"

"Benevolent."

"Aldie, can you see God?"

A sly grin and a slow nodding. "Yes."

"Where is God?"

"Right behind death."[8]

Soon after, when Connie [Aldie's stepdaughter] was on watch:

Aldie was alternately talking and listening, and Connie asked,

"Is he here?" ["he" referring to death]

"Which one?"

"Are there two?"

A slow nodding.

"Who is the second one?"

"Love. Go get mother. I have to give her some."[9]

And later:

Sometimes during the dialogue there was a sense of argument. Aldie would nod thoughtfully or say "yes" or "no," then speak with the inflection of a question, and appear to ponder the answer. Sometimes there seemed to be the energy of a crucial struggle. There was a triangular bar hanging over his head so he could raise his arms and grasp it, shifting his shoulders slightly against the bed. Once I watched as he grasped one end of it slowly in his left hand, turned it upright like a club and shook it slowly three times at the unseen presence. A victorious smile spread across his face. Later he turned to Connie who was beside the bed and said, "I'm winning. How about that?"[10]

On the final day:

The dialogue ended about two hours before his death. On the morning of the day Aldie died, we heard him say several different times, "Yes, I'm ready. Okay. Yes." Or "I'm so glad. I'm ready." He was addressing the presences he had called Death and Love, confirming and acknowledging as if an agreement had been reached.[11]

After "a long period of quiet," everyone circled about Aldie for his final passing:

We watched as he tried to draw in a final breath, but no air would come. His shoulders rose and his face twisted briefly in effort, and then relaxed. Complete stiffness.[12]

A man's life had ended. And yet, as Ginnie said, Aldie's death was "a victory." After first being diagnosed with cancer, he had stepped consciously onto Decision Road (even if he wouldn't have used those words). Then, during the last fifteen months of his life, he had done the difficult work of the Death Lodge and the Purpose Circle. When his time came to step onto the Great Ballcourt, he was more ready than most for this final dance. But for Aldie, it wasn't a dance with Death alone. He also called in God and Love.

As Meredith wrote in her journal soon after: "Death transformed through love, for the dying. Love transformed through death, for the living."[13]

The Self Emptying Itself of Self

In her book *The Grace in Dying,* Kathleen Singh suggests that the psychospiritual stages of dying do not always end with acceptance, the last of the Kübler-Ross stages.[14] Kübler-Ross describes this stage not as being a happy time, but rather as one devoid of feelings. "It is as if the pain had gone, the struggle is over, and there comes a time for 'the final rest before the long journey.'"[15] Acceptance is merely the eye of the storm.[16] The outward struggle comes to an end, but an inner discomfort still remains.

According to Singh, spiritual development may continue beyond acceptance, leading onto what she calls surrender.[17] Her description of surrender offers another perspective on what happened to Aldie in his final days. Surrender is neither giving up nor saying "there's nothing left to do." Rather, surrender is being engaged in life, releasing fully into the moment-to-moment experience of *what is.* Standing stark naked at death's door, the hope of a future forever gone, the dying person understands that all *there is* is this precious moment . . . and *this* one . . . and *this* one. "Be Here Now" is no longer a trite aphorism, a relic of the '60s and '70s. At the very end, the present moment was all that Aldie had. And to each one, he gave himself fully.

The journey from acceptance to surrender, Scott Peck has called kenosis, "the process of the self emptying itself of self, of the ego bumping itself off."[18] The word kenosis, of Greek derivation, means *an emptying* and has been used in Christianity to refer to Christ's self-renunciation of divine nature so that he could take on the form of man. When used to describe a spiritual transformation at the end of life, kenosis means much the opposite. What is emptied are limiting images of the self, which allows a present-tense connection to the divine, whatever name a person may have for it: God, Love, Spirit, or the Ground of Being. The self empties itself of self that the person might become one with *All That Is.*

Surrender is not only a potential stage for the person who is dying. Total surrender is the great longing of the spiritual seeker, the person who wants to lose the shackles of self-identification in order to know God, who is Love, which is the Transcendent. This is Christ wandering in the desert, the Buddha meditating under the Bodhi tree, or the modern-day ascetic sitting alone in a monastery. More modestly, this is the everyday person who steps away from the rush of the modern world and surrenders to a ceremony of renewal in the desert. This is the person who is learning to die in order to live.

Good Death, Bad Death . . . My Death

Aldie's dying is a quintessential example of "the good death:" a poignant end that was deeply fulfilling. His "victory" was made possible by the many blessings he received. Time enough to wrap up business affairs. Final days at home in his own bed. Surrounded by loving family and friends. Supported by skilled and compassionate professionals. Physical symptoms controlled well enough by medicines. Flashes of clarity so he could say his final goodbyes. And freedom to dance inside, to work out his final relationship with Love, Death, and God.

Take away one of these key elements and another person's death might not seem such a victory. Take away a number of them and a quintessential version of "the bad death" might result. For some of these unlucky people, the primary cause of suffering will be physical, be it pain, nausea, or some other hard-to-control symptom. For others, a difficult dying is not just the result of physical problems, but rather the end to an already troubled life. For the person not given the time or the means to heal important relationships, or the person whose life has brought despair more than a sense of integrity, the final dance with death may be a dizzying spin with old karmic ghosts. Isolation and anguish. Anger and blame. Bitterness and regret. Guilt and remorse. Loneliness and pain. Whatever their names, these old ghosts may allow little room on the Great Ballcourt for reconciling with God, embracing Love, or surrendering to Death.

Describing the extremes of the good death and the bad death can be deeply evocative. These contrasting images accentuate the importance of doing Death Lodge and Purpose Circle work *right now,* while each of us is still alive and well. But notions of good or bad can also lead to dangerous self-criticism. If someone does not have the time or the capacity for a final working through—be it with God, Love, Death, or Whomever—does it mean that person has failed? The very question suggests that death and a judgment day are inevitably linked, an idea with a long history in Western culture. Another option may be for each person to ask: *How can I make this death of mine my very own? How can that final dance on the Great Ballcourt be a unique and essential expression of "all of me?"*

Steven had his own ideas about the good death and the bad death. He often spoke or wrote about his determination to die well, if only for the sake of his family.

> Now I see that I must make a work of art of my life, as a legacy for those living souls who will soon follow. Now I see that I am dying for those who are living.
> . . . I vow to fight for quality, cracked and earthen vessel that I am, quality in life and quality in death. The American Indian term for death is 'the giveaway.' I will give my life to death so that my people will prosper, so that my kind can survive and my children will be blessed.[19]

But Steven's own version of the good death would have to be . . . *his own version.* For him, life had always been about brutal honesty and fierce attachment. No borders, no boundaries. Whatever came his way, he would open to it, grasp at it, and come to know it—with all the passion he could muster. At times, this urgency *to know* led him to stare at the sun for just a little too long. More than once he seared his retinas, but he also saw glorious sights that many of us will never know. His approach to death would be no different.

While walking with a friend a few short years before his death, Steven encountered the maggot-ridden corpse of a coyote. With death already made real by every hacking cough, every rasping breath, Steven stared at the carcass as if it were his own.

> The foul stench of death solidified into a carcass swarming with maggots moving across it in waves, like stalks of wheat across a field in the wind. The New Age healing guru doesn't talk about maggots. She doesn't talk about death memory.
>
> Who wants to talk about the memory that pulls us inexorably towards the reality of our being? Elias and I stood for a long time, looking at those busy little maggots. Our knees shook. We were trying to observe them with the artist's eye, to see the beauty. But such beauty is never unaccompanied by a shudder, a knowing, a remembering.[20]

Even with his unbridled passion, Steven didn't carry great projections about an afterlife, be they fantasies or fears. For him, death was the natural and inevitable end to life. It wasn't "romantic," it certainly wasn't "pretty," but neither was it "a failure."

> The roaring of the blood, the roaring of life, hardly give the living enough quietude to be aware of the proximity of their own death. I disagree with the New Age healer [who writes that all of us can heal ourselves if we just try]. I challenge her to be aware of the roaring of her blood. It is not the blood that thunders. It is the collective voice of all the maggots. In the pounding their words can be heard. They are saying "We are God. We are the mind that threads through the entire universe. We are the end and the beginning. We are death. And we are life." I challenge her to look into her own shadow and stop begging the question. Death does not come because it's a symptom of our "victimness." Death comes because it is death, because it is the very body of life, because we have to be born. Death comes because we love life too much. Death comes because, like everything from galaxies to proteins, we have to die.

"Beauty is truth and truth beauty," said Keats. Beauty is the maggots. Truth is the memory of the maggots. That's where I'm going. To the land of beauty and truth.[21]

Choosing a Sacred Weapon

In the Northern Cheyenne teachings offered by Hyemeyohsts Storm, the dying person brings to the Great Ballcourt a lifetime of virtues and faults.[22] The Ballcourt, though, is a place of perfect balance. The virtues a person carries onto the court will be mirrored by their negative opposites, and the faults will be matched by their positive reflections, too. Before the dance begins, said Storm, a dying person is encouraged to choose a "sacred weapon," the most essential quality that will best serve the person during this trial. Like everything else on the Ballcourt, though, the weapon that is chosen will be met by its opposite. But be reassured, this final game on the Ballcourt is not about winning or losing. With life soon to end, this is a chance for the dying person to make a final peace. The poet Rilke said: "the wish to have a death of one's own is growing ever rarer."[23] But it is here on the Great Ballcourt, sacred weapon in hand, that we each have a chance to do just that.

What sacred weapon shall be mine? A question like that fascinated Steven far more than most people. In 1984, a few years after first hearing Storm's teaching, he wrote in his journal, "Could it be that <u>breath</u> will be my sacred weapon when I enter the Great Ballcourt?"[24] He wrote these words within weeks of the first journal entry that hinted he already had a breathing problem. His death was still nearly twenty years away.

For Steven, *breath* was much the same as *spirit*. "'Spirit' I can understand easily enough," he wrote the year before he died. "Because my lungs are the cause of my distress, I can locate spirit in my breathing. As long as I can breathe in and out, I am spirit. When I cease to breathe in and out, spirit goes elsewhere."[25] *Breath* and *spirit* made possible his words of inspiration; the inspired word encouraged him to give and receive stories; and the giving and receiving of stories had been his greatest passion. In his living, *breath* and *spirit* truly had been Steven's sacred weapon. And so, too, would it be in his dying.

Following the teachings from Storm, if *breath* was Steven's sacred weapon, then its opposite, *no breath,* would also be called onto the Great Ballcourt. In his later years, *no breath* would become Steven's companion, the Dark Goddess that visited him almost nightly. After years of dancing with her, he wrote to a friend months before he died, "The dying process is rich and full and a fucking bitch."[26] The suffocation terror of *no breath* was far worse than what most dying people would ever know. Truly a fucking bitch. And yet with his *breath*—which is *spirit,* which means the capacity to be *inspired*—Steven was able to transform these terrible changes into something rich and full. If his great gift in life was to be inspired, to be full of *breath,* then *no breath* forced Steven to come to terms with his own mortality, the certainty of his own extinction. In Meredith's words, this dancing with *breath* and *no breath* became "the final honing of Steven's soul, taking him into areas of acceptance he might never have reached."[27]

This constant twirling with *breath* and *no breath* also gave Steven a premonition of his final crossing. It came to him while he was fasting alone in the Confidence Hills of Death Valley. On the second day out, the desert whipped up a dust storm, making it almost impossible for his weakened lungs to breathe. He climbed into a sleeping bag, his only protection, and made a breathing hole no larger than an egg. There he lay for hours.

> It was then I saw my end. First will come the wind to fill my lungs with particles of death. There will be no way to avoid this insinuation. Twist and thrash as I will, my breath will take my soul through. In-out, in-out—*in . . . out . . .*
>
> Then there will be a great calm. Everything will become crystal clear. *. . . In . . . Out.*[28]

The Last Breath of Life

When exactly does a person die? Is the moment of death the last exhalation, the final heartbeat, or the point when cellular damage is irreversible? Or is it something more enigmatic, that indefinable moment when "the soul" leaves the body?

In the world of science, a distinction is made between clinical death and biological death. With clinical death, all external signs of life are absent. Metabolism may continue at the cellular level, but if the organism is not revived within minutes, clinical death will soon be followed by irreversible biological death. In a hospital, where a Code Blue might bring someone back to life, this distinction is critically important. But for people who decline such extreme measures, especially those who die at home without monitors, this distinction will likely be meaningless. "Death" will simply be the cessation of *all* that constitutes life: consciousness, breath, heartbeat, reflexes, and cellular function. That one of these ceases seconds or minutes before another will matter little.

During a vigil at home, the primary sign that death is imminent is often a change in respirations. This may include periods of heavy breathing, shallow breathing, or long stretches of no breathing. A weakened cough may make it difficult for the dying person to clear lung secretions, leading to a loud, raspy "death rattle." A more pronounced use of rib cage muscles may also occur, sometimes signaling the last few breaths just before death.

If the dying person is already unconscious, caregivers and witnesses who stay for the vigil are often subdued, if not silent, causing these breathing changes to become more pronounced. For some, the look and sound of this final breathing will be terrifying. For people more able to be present with what is, the sound may transform the bedroom into a place as sacred as any temple or church. According to Hildegard of Bingen, "prayer is nothing but inhaling and exhaling the one breath of the Universe, which is ruler and spirit. There's only one spirit but there are many souls."[29]

Imagine again your own final dying. Perhaps the people who have come to hold vigil will be able to share with you a special kind of communion. Though different souls, together you will inhale and exhale the one spirit that is All Life. To make this connection real and explicit, your family and friends may hold your hand, cradle your head, or massage your feet. They may even breathe along with you for a time, matching out-breath with out-breath, in-breath with in-breath. With each exhalation, together you die. With each inhalation, together you are reborn. The cycle of death-and-rebirth is reduced to its most elemental form.

But soon comes the time for parting company. Room for many, then room for a few, now room only for one. You take a few last breaths and then . . . nothing. Nothing but silence. No movement of air. No communion with All Life. Something—some *thing*—has disappeared from your body. The religious might call it "the soul." Scientists might call it "life force." Whatever it was that once animated your physical body—the "you" that made you unique and irreplaceable—is now gone.

What Lies Beyond?

Where does that "you" or "me" or "Steven" go from here? A mystery. A mystery answerable only when the time comes for each of us to step onto, and then out of, the Great Ballcourt.

Is that dance with death an absolute end? Or is there something more beyond, be it heaven, hell, or someplace intermediate? Or will each of us be reincarnated back on Earth?

In centuries past, these questions were answered by whichever group mythology a person inherited, with all of these old mythologies suggesting that death was not an absolute end. For the first time in human history, however, large numbers of modern people do not have a comfort story about the afterlife. "This is it," many might say. "When I die, I'm dead. No Heaven, no Hell. No resurrection, no reincarnation." A scientific view says that we die, we decay, and then our remains are reabsorbed into the compost of the earth. Life may still follow death, but only as organic building blocks for other organisms, not as the perpetuation of a single person's soul. And yet, judging from the long history of afterlife stories, the human psyche yearns for a myth about rebirth. Without such a story, the modern scientist or skeptic is left with an existential angst not so easy to resolve.

Whatever your own beliefs may be, your dying will be a journey: a crossing from this world to whatever lies beyond, even if what's beyond is annihilation. A common metaphor in deathbed language is travel, including images of boats, trains, cars, passports, or tickets.[30] It's as if people were struggling to figure out what needs to be left behind, what is needed for the journey across, and what is waiting for them on the other side. When your own dying time comes, you, too, will draw upon personal ideas and images about the final crossing, and with them you will do your own working through.

Raised in a fundamentalist family, Steven left behind Christian notions of an afterlife soon after becoming an adult. He did not have any definite beliefs about what comes after death, but neither did he dismiss afterlife ideas as nonsense. More than anything, Steven was a visionary poet who was fascinated by some of life's greatest metaphors: symbolic death, physical death, and life-after-death. Perhaps his most telling evocation of these themes is the final words of *We Who Have Gone Before,* a book finished a year before his death.

I have never been frightened when darkness fell. I welcomed it with an open heart. I do not think one could find anything more beautiful than the appearance of stars in the sky, or the rising of the full moon on the eastern horizon. Yet when I came close to dying, I did not want to be left alone in a dark room.

I will try to rise and go into the next room, where lights are burning with the promise of life. I may even try to go toward that ineluctable delight, but will be unable to rise. What then? Will the stars come out, one by one? Will the familiar constellations appear? Will my eyes follow the outlines of the Great Bear to the North Star? Or will I close them against the oncoming night and wish I'd never been born?

Sometimes it seems everybody has an opinion about "where I am going"—everybody but me. The closer I get, the less I seem to know. All I know for certain is that darkness will fall. And then the stars will appear.[31]

The Final Crossing

Alpha One

There's a wall I'm trying to get over
breath-climbing inch by inch
       banana peel fingers and toes
and I keep slipping back into
going up
not wanting to
desperately not wanting to
fall

every night
I slip between the covers of death
my woman's chest rises and falls
steady as a clock
no mountain for her to climb
she sleeps so easily
little boat floating on the water
fair winds and an endless sea

while on all fours
like a mountaineer I cling
with imaginary ropes and pitons
to that imaginary wall

they say dolphins breathe consciously
dying by
deliberately choosing to drown

can it be that death has invited me
to be a conscious breather
to climb that slippery wall

while all around me
love dreams ocean dreams
in ebbs and flows and tides of air
while I, not wanting to
desperately not wanting to,
fall [1]

– Steven Foster

The Final Crossing

Tuesday, May 6

So where does this visit lead? Where am I headed after this, the last home visit? *Steven is dying. Meredith is becoming a widow. And Scott is . . .*

I ease off the accelerator just slightly as the bridge begins to slope down, heading toward the opposite shore.

Arriving. That's it! Scott is fully arriving, bringing "all of me" to the bedside to do this work. *Yes, I'm arriving.*

A half hour later, I reach Steven and Meredith's home. Parking my car at the top of the driveway, I get out and begin walking down the long, curving driveway. My mind begins to focus on what's ahead by recalling all the recent phone calls with Meredith that updated me about Steven.

In five days, everything has changed. The night after the last visit, Meredith gave Steven a combination of Thorazine and occasional morphine to good effect. The monsters receded and Steven was able to sleep. By the next night, though, he was running fevers, coughing more, and breathing even harder. His cold likely had turned into pneumonia. Again, he refused to go to the hospital, so we started antibiotics and increased his steroids. When his oxygen levels dipped a few days later, I arranged for another tank to be delivered so we could double the flow of oxygen. That would be the last desperate attempt to help him rally.

Everything we can offer Steven at home is now here. Everything except hospice. They aren't scheduled to come until tomorrow. *Probably too late.*

At the end of the driveway, I pass through the front gate into the open courtyard. With no trees overhead and the storm clouds gone, there is only blue sky. Walking by the main house, I see no sign of

Meredith's parents, so I continue across the deck. At the top of the outdoor staircase, I pause one last time.

Months ago, Steven asked me to be boatman for his final crossing, his last rite of passage. In a home death, though, the role of Charon is usually played by an entire hospice team, not a single person, and certainly not a physician. "All of me" will have to include some unfamiliar roles: not just doctor, but nurse, social worker, chaplain, maybe even home health aide. *A hospice team all-in-one. Am I ready for this?*

I recall the moment when my pre-visit fear reached its peak on the Golden Gate Bridge, a half hour earlier. Strangely, though, the fear is now gone. No racing thoughts, no twisting sensation in the stomach.

"All of me" present to do this work. What might that mean? I am about to enter a sacred place. Once inside, what am I supposed to do? Nothing. At first, do nothing. I take in a deep breath and let it out slowly. *Just stay close. Listen. Be an empty vessel. And lead with service.*

After descending the stairs, I knock three times on the door and let myself in.

In the center of the room is Steven, his large body seated on the corner of the bed, surrounded by Meredith, her closest friend, Gigi, and two other people I haven't met. Steven's legs are on the floor, his torso leaning way forward, arms resting on a table, forehead pressing against a large headrest made of solid foam. He's wearing sweatpants and a black T-shirt. I can't see the front of it, but I'm sure I know which one it is.

Steven seems oblivious to my entrance, the only indication he's alive being the rhythmic heaving of his chest. Coming closer, I see that most of his weight is being held up by the table and the foam block, none of it by his own strength. *He's unconscious,* I tell myself.

Unconscious. The condition begs a few age-old questions: Is a person in a coma aware of the people around him? Does Steven understand anything of words being spoken? Deep inside, does he at least sense what others are feeling? Especially Meredith—the grief she holds, her anticipation of what's to come, and her fear of the unknown.

Meredith gets up to greet me, offering a gentle kiss and embrace. She introduces me to Selene, Steven and Meredith's twenty-five year old daughter, who is sitting beside Steven, and then to Jay, Meredith's brother, who is standing off to the side. I say hello to both of them, then exchange an embrace with Gigi, whom I already know. Each person seems fully present, but very subdued. *Is it exhaustion,* I wonder, *or respect for what is sacred? Probably both.*

I go over to the other side of Steven, the space vacated by Meredith, and sit down. "Hello Steven," I say softly into his ear, my hand resting on his back. "It's Scott. I've come to be with you."

No movement, no acknowledgement. Just the next big rise of his barrel chest, his breath now merely a reflex.

What part of Steven is still alive? I wonder. *And what part is already dead?* Gone are his incisive, rambling mind and that bigger-than-life personality. *But what about his cracked-open heart?*

As I rub his back gently, I am overtaken by a sudden expectation *to do* something. *Come on,* I chide myself, *you're a doctor.* But little do I know that I've already done what is most important: I have arrived. The simple act of my arrival, Meredith will tell me later, has relieved her of all extraneous roles, especially that of nurse. She is now able to be just Steven's wife.

Seeing a single scopolamine patch behind Steven's ear makes me realize how raucous his breathing sounds.

He's not "drowning," I tell myself, *but the noise is probably upsetting to the others.*

Speaking to no one in particular, I suggest a second patch be put on. Gigi is a step ahead of Meredith, getting another one from a box of medicines and placing it behind Steven's other ear.

I ask Meredith about the last dose of morphine. She tells me when it was given and how Steven responded.

"Then we can wait awhile for the next dose," I tell her.

There now, you've done something. Now just sit for awhile. Sit here and take in all the signs.

His breathing . . .

Another guttural heave of an in-breath, then a slower out-breath like a muffled snore. A silent pause, then another big heave followed by a release. Each is the same as the one before, each triggered by an animal reflex from deep within the primordial brain.

His face . . .

The oxygen mask and the foam block are hiding much of it, but as I look from the side, I see no sign of a grimace suggesting pain or discomfort.

His body . . .

Except for the heaving chest, no movement whatsoever. No struggle, no fight.

The smell . . .

A faint musty odor, probably stale sweat, but nothing pungent like urine or feces.

The sounds . . .

Steven's wet, raspy breath, backed by the noise of the oxygen machines.

Two machines, not just one, I recall. Though hidden away in a small, separate kitchen, they make an incessant noise that fills the room. *Clearly he's dying,* I tell myself, *but with all that oxygen, this could go on for a long time. With oxygen, hours, maybe even another day. Without oxygen, probably minutes.*

I remember the phone call I had with Meredith from the night before. Her words then said it all: "No clear communication . . . increasing agitation . . . more confusion." *The final crossing is fast approaching,* I told myself, realizing almost immediately what that final boat ride would likely require. "If his condition doesn't improve," I told her, "eventually we may want to remove the oxygen." I paused to let these words sink in. "It may be the best way to make his dying gentle and easy."

Time has come to prepare for the crossing, I tell myself. *But step-by-step. First, speak with Meredith. Alone.*

I usher her over to the entrance foyer. In the shadows of that small space, I can't see her face. Still, I can sense her strength and her resolve. She's determined to do what's right, what's needed, what will serve this ceremony. *Running on the energy of that ceremony alone,* I tell myself. *Soon enough, she'll collapse.*

"So tell me what's been happening," I ask her.

"Yesterday afternoon, Steven began drifting in and out . . ." She continues, giving a detailed account of all that's happened since, speaking more softly than usual. During an evening visit from his son

Keenan, and Keenan's wife and daughter, Steven made an extraordinary effort to greet them well, only to slip away again. Then a long and restless night began, with erratic sleep punctuated by terrible bouts of *no breath*. Around four o'clock in the morning, during one of the worst stretches, Steven suddenly stood upright as if he could just walk away from all the suffering, only to fall back in bed with both arms outstretched. After that, he finally slept for a few hours. His daughter Selene arrived around eight o'clock and to her he spoke his last word, "Selene!"

Throughout the morning Steven remained restless, unable to talk, yet also unable to relax or drift away. Having been taught the easiest way to breathe—sitting up and leaning forward over a table— he wasn't willing to leave that position. Whenever the others would try to lay him back in the bed, he would fight. And yet he wasn't strong enough to hold himself up, so they each took turns straddling him from behind.

"Exhausting physical work," Meredith explains. "Like labor. Steven's always wondered what it would be like to give birth. Well, this has been physical labor, just like when Selene was born. Now it's Steven's turn. He's giving birth, releasing himself from the womb of his body."

Meredith continues talking, focusing on the details of the story, getting them just right. Somehow "the facts" help to orient her, to keep her on track. Her voice wavers only once, when she describes the last time Steven looked at her knowingly, around ten o'clock that morning.

"He stared at me with these infinite eyes." Her voice cracks. "Right at me. No words, but the look alone said it all. *This is it,* he seemed to say, *I'm dying. I am <u>here</u>. I am dying. I <u>see</u> you and I love you.*"

She pauses for the longest time, fighting back tears.

"Only in the last hour or so have we all begun to settle," she says, trying to ground herself in more recent events. "First, Jay set up that headrest, so his position could be more stable. Then morphine seemed to help him to relax. And with that, the rest of us could relax, too."

"Any sign of pain? Moaning, grimacing, anything like that?"

"No, not really. Just that breathing. That awful sound, like he's drowning. It's gotten better since we talked on the phone, but still it sounds horrible."

"I know the breathing sounds bad," I explain, "but the noisiness doesn't worry me so much. It's just another sign that he's nearing the end. Is he still suffering? That's the big question. For Steven, suffering has always meant shortness of breath more than pain. But as long as he's not fighting, moaning, or grimacing, then it's unlikely he's feeling any suffocation. It would be great to dry up those secretions more, but more important is the coma and the morphine. With those two working together, we can make this peaceful for him."

Her face seems to relax, if only slightly. Or is it only my imagination? I want to believe I am helping her, too, but easing her suffering is a much harder task. Steven will leave his body soon enough. For a long time, though, Meredith will have to carry inside her the pain of this day.

"Meredith, time we speak again about the oxygen, like we did last night." Our eyes lock momentarily, then release. "Steven's nearing the end, but he could still hang on for quite a while. Question is: How do we best relieve his suffering? How do we release him from his body?"

She nods her head, not yet ready to speak.

"If we stop the oxygen," I explain, "he'll probably die within minutes. With it still on, he could linger for hours. But there's no rush for any of this. Only when you're ready. Only when everyone here is ready."

I wait and still no response. She obviously needs time for her heart and mind to become one, for all the thoughts and feelings to commingle. Love. Fear. Release. Grief. Goodbye.

"I understand," she finally says, nodding her head again. She looks directly at me. "Can you explain this to the others? I've already spoken about it with Gigi, but not with Selene or Jay."

"How about if I tell Steven? I'll tell Steven and the others can hear it, too."

"Yeah, that's good. Tell Steven."

Together we return to the main room with Meredith leading the way. She goes off to a corner and leans against the wall, standing in that one-legged egret posture of hers. I head over to Steven's right side and sit on the bed.

"Steven, it's Scott again." My hand rubs his back while I search for just the right tone—gentle, yet loud enough for everyone to hear. "This is it, Steven, the final crossing. You're dying. It's time now to ferry you to the other side. I want to tell you what I see and how I think I can help."

I pause and wait for a reaction. No response.

"I want this trip to be as peaceful as possible. We have morphine here, which has always worked well for you. We'll make sure you get what you need from that. No more suffocation. No more terror. I promise."

I can't see everyone in the room, but I sense they are all listening, all fully present.

"Steven, you've always been so clear that you didn't want any last-minute heroics." I list all the interventions he's declined over the last months: specialists, hospitals, X-rays, blood tests. "Now, I imagine, you wouldn't even want the oxygen. Not if it's going to prolong the suffering. Not if it'll make this crossing even longer than it needs to be. If we continue the oxygen, this could go on for hours. If we stop it, probably five or ten minutes."

I pause again, this time scanning the room. I see no visible reaction from the others, so I return my focus to Steven.

"You've always said you weren't afraid of death. That it was the dying that frightened you. Well, time now to make that dying as gentle as possible . . . as peaceful as possible."

Still no facial response, just the gurgling breath. No purposeful movement, just the heaving of his chest.

"But first, Steven, time to say goodbye. Time to say the biggest 'thank you' possible. A 'thank you' for all that you've given me."

Forgiveness, gratitude, love, and goodbye are the final steps for completing a relationship, but our short time as friends has been so clean that there's really nothing to forgive. *May not be true for the others,* I tell myself. *Seldom is.*

"Steven, I know you've heard me say this before, but again, it's been such a huge honor and privilege to know you, to serve as your doctor. One of the greatest of my life. The experience has filled me for months. I expect it will fill me for some time to come. Thank you. Thank you for all of that."

I close my eyes, searching inside for what else I have to say. A bitterness, almost anger, suddenly wells up inside. Yes, I do feel incredibly blessed to have known this man, but I also feel ripped off. After only four visits, something precious is being stolen away. *So forgiveness is needed. Forgiveness for his dying so soon.*

"Steven, my greatest regret is that we didn't have more time together. That we didn't have a chance to discover more about what lay between us. But still, I relish the time we've had. You're the one who said it first. 'Yes, doc,' you wrote me once, 'if you must know, I love you.' Well, dear Steven, I love you, too. More than you know, I love you. Goodbye, dear friend."

With little of his face visible, I lean over and kiss his cheek. Stepping back, I look over to Meredith, making room for her to take her place at Steven's side.

"Oh, my love," Meredith begins, her voice at once soft, yet solid. "What you've given to me has been so big. In love, in children, in work, in so much pain and joy. Always bold, always real, always totally human. Thank you for this incredible life we've had. For being my teacher, my lover, my partner. I won't stop loving you. Ever."

With the word *ever,* her voice cracks again. She pauses to collect herself, but now the tears are flowing steadily.

"You are so beautiful, so brave. Go where you need to go, and trust that I will be alright. I'll find my way. Wherever you go, you will always be with me. Death won't stop my love for you. It's hard to let you go, but I must. And I am ready. I want you out of this pain. Oh how I have loved you. Nothing will ever take that from me, or from you. Forever, my love."

One by one, the others come forth. Gigi speaks of captive dolphins being released to the sea, and Steven being released to another world. Selene, a daughter able to see beyond the mythic figure inflated by so many others, offers love to her real-life father, a man whose love for her was never questioned. And Jay, brother-in-law, a man soon to be married, tells him how much he regrets that Steven will miss the wedding, but how grateful he is for the way Steven has already witnessed and blessed the relationship.

After Jay, the room becomes silent, everyone soon lost in the time warp of a dying vigil. Seconds might be minutes; minutes might be hours. It doesn't really matter. It's not about slow or fast, not about past or future, not about remembering what's happened or anticipating what's to come. It's just the present moment. One present moment after another. Stretching on and on into the dusk of this long day.

The intensity of it all eventually becomes too much to bear. None of us can watch and witness every rise of Steven's chest, every fall. One person fidgets. Someone else moves to a new vantage point in the room. Another steps outside for a break. But always a few people remain at Steven's side, there to keep the vigil, ready to bear witness to his inevitable passing.

When it's Meredith who gets up to leave the room, I suddenly become more alert. *Time again to speak,* I tell myself.

I give her a few minutes alone and then follow behind, finding her just outside the door, smoking a cigarette. We look directly into each other's eyes. In the warm light of the afternoon, I now see the exhaustion that's etched on her face. I know she knows what I'm about to say, still the words must be spoken.

"There's no rush, Meredith . . . but whenever you're ready."

"Okay," she says. She betrays none of the emotions that are swirling inside. Only the fatigue is obvious. "But first, let me go walk with it for a while."

I nod my head, offer a gentle embrace and release her. I release her to the walk and to the hardest decision she will make in a very long time, perhaps ever.

Minutes later, Meredith returns. Without hesitation, she walks over to Gigi first. "I think it's time to let him go. Any doubts from you?"

"No," Gigi says, "I'll support whatever you do."

Meredith looks next to Selene and then to Jay. No words, no flinching. Everyone seems to be ready.

She looks at me last and nods her head.

"First, let's give him some morphine. He's due now anyway."

Meredith, so used to being Steven's nurse, reaches for the medicine bottle. I choose to stay back, though prepared to step forward if I see the slightest hesitation.

Once the morphine is administered, we return to waiting. This time, though, we have a clear goal. We're waiting for the morphine to seep through the mucosa in his mouth, into the bloodstream and onto the brain. We're waiting for it to attach to special receptors in the pain center, which is also the place that blocks breathlessness. Most of all, we're waiting for the relaxation and relief it will bring to Steven.

My own mind again is active—thinking, planning, anticipating. Again I'm preparing to do something. *First, we'll need to get him on his back.* I recall Meredith's description of the physical battles earlier in the day. Any sign of struggle with repositioning would likely mean he's still capable of suffering. *If none of that happens, only then do we turn off the oxygen.*

After untold minutes, an internal clock tells me that our waiting on the morphine is over. I ask Jay to help me lift Steven back into bed. I am surprised just how heavy his body is. *A body big enough for such a large spirit,* I tell myself. *But now the body is dead weight.*

Jay and I hold Steven in an upright position on the edge of the bed, while the others move the table away and then pile pillows on the bed behind him. We lift Steven a little and slide him back into a stable, reclining position. Through it all, Steven offers no response. No moaning. No furrowed brow. No physical resistance.

I look around at the others, one at a time, searching for any sign of reluctance. I see none. *The time has come,* I tell myself.

I follow the oxygen tubing around the corner to where the machines are hidden in the kitchenette. I know what needs to be done, but still I feel uneasy. *Like the Wizard of Oz,* I suddenly realize. A small, nondescript man, hidden behind a screen, wielding godlike powers, yet vulnerable to easy detection. No time to back out now.

I turn off one of the two oxygen tanks and walk back into the room to survey the scene. I don't expect anything to be different and it isn't. Back behind the wizard's screen, I start slowly turning off the second tank, five liters to three, and a little later, three liters to one. I check back in the room, but still no change. I return to the oxygen and turn it off completely.

Rejoining the vigil, I watch each of the others first, seeing no sign of distress among them. I then join them all in focusing on Steven's every breath. A sudden heave of the chest . . . a slow, gurgling exhale . . . a pause. Another heave . . . exhale . . . pause. Over and over, the pattern continues. One after the other, each the same as before. Time counted out, breath by breath.

As we watch, I recall a weeklong meditation retreat I attended recently. One of the teachers was trying to inspire the participants to stay focused on each and every breath, using it as a central anchor for this mindfulness practice. "Return to the miracle of your first breath," he told us, "when you first were delivered from your mother's womb." He paused to allow each person to conjure up this image. "Now imagine that future day when you'll be on your deathbed. Imagine yourself taking your very last breath, preparing to leave your body." Again he paused. "No great difficulty being present for each of those breaths, yes? So imagine that every single breath you take is as miraculous as that first one. Every single breath is as precious as the last one. Give each and every one of them your fullest attention."

And so we all do this together with Steven. Every single out-breath is a dying. Every single in-breath is a rebirth. . . . *out* . . . *in* . . . *out* . . . *in* . . .

About a quarter of an hour later, I begin to worry. *How long will this go on?* I remember what I said earlier—"probably five or ten minutes"—and then I cringe. I broke one of the cardinal rules of hospice care, a rule I've taught to countless physicians. When declaring a prognosis, *never* give a number.

What should I have said? I ask myself. *With oxygen, hours, maybe days. Without oxygen, minutes, maybe hours.* I feel my stomach turning over for the first time since crossing the Golden Gate Bridge.

I say nothing to the others, but soon everyone understands. Waiting for Steven to die *in minutes* gradually shifts to waiting *for hours*. Jay is the first to declare the new phase of the vigil. He goes to a nearby shelf, leafing through different books until he settles on one. He is obviously engaged with a passage, so Selene encourages him to read it aloud. Her suggestion energizes Jay, making him stand a little straighter, bringing a smile to his face. Finally there is something *to do,* something that will honor Steven. He begins reading from Wordsworth's "Intimations of Immortality," his voice growing in volume and filling the room.

Inspired by Jay, Selene goes to the bookshelf herself. "Blake was his favorite," she declares with confidence, as she pulls out a thick volume. She flips through it and then settles on "The Tyger" from *Songs of Experience.* Her voice is strong like Jay's, suggesting a sense of pride, but it's also seductively sweet. When she finishes, everyone shifts back to watching Steven's breathing.

. . . out . . . in . . . out . . . in . . . Still no change.

Minutes later, I see one of Steven's own books, *We Who Have Gone Before,* sitting on a nearby counter. I pick it up knowing exactly what to read.

"I have never been frightened when darkness fell. I welcomed it with an open heart . . ."

I read the last three paragraphs of the book with a careful diction and a measured pace.

". . . Sometimes it seems everybody has an opinion about 'where I am going'—everybody but me. The closer I get, the less I seem to know. All I know for certain is that darkness will fall. And then the stars will appear."

"That would be Steven Foster," I conclude. Staring outside to a dimly lit forest, I realize that darkness will be coming soon.

Sometime later I look at a nearby clock, wondering how long it's been since the oxygen was turned off. *An hour? Maybe two?*

Time for more morphine, I decide. *But leave Meredith out of it this time. Let her be the grieving spouse.*

"It's been a while since the last dose," I tell the others. I measure out twenty milligrams of the morphine and then place it into the side of his mouth.

Again we wait, this time without any clear goal. Another breath . . . and then another. Present moment after present moment. Occasionally a pause between two of Steven's breaths is longer than usual. *Is this the end?* But then another breath starts and the old rhythm returns.

"It's like an all-night vigil during a four-day fast," I say to Meredith. "You've been awake forever, waiting for the sunrise, but it seems like it'll never come."

She smiles back, understanding what I mean.

The comment stirs me somehow, renewing my connection to Steven. Without a reason, without a plan, I go over and sit beside him. I am by his head, with the length of his body stretching out to my right. Leaning forward, I place my hand on his chest and start rubbing his breastbone. Perhaps it's just something *to do,* but this *doing* connects me even more to Steven, to his breathing and to each present moment.

How appropriate, I tell myself, recalling the hand-on-chest gesture I first learned in a Death Valley base-camp. Slow, gentle circles connecting me to him, him to me. *I'm in base-camp again, but this time as lead guide.*

Still rubbing his chest, I lower my face so I can whisper in his right ear. My head is now so close to his, I could almost rest my forehead on his forehead.

"Easy with the breathing, Steven," I tell him softly. "Slow and easy. Relax into each breath. No struggle, no fear. Just slow, easy breathing. Time to make this crossing smooth and gentle." Over and over, I repeat words similar to these. His breathing takes the lead. I follow. No sign of change comes. Maybe minutes go by, me still rubbing his chest and whispering.

Then the pattern of breathing starts to shift. *Could this really be it?* I wonder. *No, I'm imagining it.*

But soon it's clear. He's definitely changing. The heave of his chest becomes ever gentler, the moist sound ever quieter. The pauses in-between become longer and longer. *We've finally reached the other side of the river,* I tell myself. *Time to step to the back of the boat. Room now only for family. Soon only for Steven.*

I stand up and gesture to Meredith to take my place. Meredith, the final guide, sits down beside Steven. The others come in closer, too, forming a circle around the two of them.

Stepping away from the group, I reach in my pocket and pull out the bag with the pfennig. *Paid in full and now my job is over.* I go to the room's corner and sit down alone.

Meredith slowly rubs Steven's chest and whispers quietly in his ear. "At last, my love, you've learned the ultimate lesson of surrender." His last few breaths are as soft and easy as any he's had in years. When finally "Steven" is gone, all that remains on his face is a look of peace with a quizzical wrinkle on the brow.

"I'm not afraid of Death," Steven once said. "No, it's the dying that scares me." But the final dying he so feared was not a hell after all. The hell had already come and gone. That hell was the years, the months, and the last few days that he had to survive just to get to Death's door. But at the very end, for the last few hours, the Dark Goddess was gentle and kind. After all his great struggles, Steven was blessed with a bit of grace—this gentle crossing.

From where I sit, off in the far corner of the room, I see none of his final exit. Alone, I stare out at the cathedral of redwoods. I am filled with awe, an uncommon sense of wonder. *What just happened? What have I witnessed? Where has Steven gone?*

Outside, the forest is much darker. Evening is fast descending. *Have no fear of the dark,* I tell myself. *Soon the stars will appear.*

Afterword

It is now three years later—almost three years to the day. As I write, I am away on another wilderness retreat, this time in the high desert of the Inyo Mountains at nearly 8,000 feet. Looking west I can see across the Owens Valley to the snow-covered Sierra. To the east is the great expanse of Eureka Valley, which spreads out to the Last Chance Mountains. North are the White Mountains and south are the rest of the Inyos. I am sitting on the top of the world, or so it seems.

I am here in base-camp, co-leading a program called "the Great Ballcourt Initiation Fast." Today is the first day of the four-day solo and scattered across a harsh, rocky landscape are eleven people who have just started to fast. A few of them have chosen to be fully exposed, making their private camps on the side of a nearby peak; others have found more limited views on lower ridges covered with pinyon pines and juniper trees; and some have hidden themselves inside closed-in washes. Each person has carried out a most valuable possession: a lifestory that is looking to be renewed. Today is the day of Decision Road, a time to turn fully into the symbolic death that soon will come. That road will lead them to a Death Lodge on the second day and a Purpose Circle on the evening of the third. Late that night, they will "die," awakening the fourth morning for a day in between worlds, a day for dancing on the Great Ballcourt. At sunrise of the fifth day they will be "reborn," returning soon after to base-camp.

My job, which I share with a co-guide, is a privileged one. Having carefully prepared the group over three full days, we are holding the center pole of base-camp, ensuring that each person returns safely. Soon we will welcome them back with an elaborate meal and then, over two full days, we will hear all their stories. My teaching partner is Meredith Little.

My one-on-one relationship with Meredith didn't begin—couldn't begin—until after Steven had died. Minutes after he had taken his last breath, she sat on the floor directly in front of me to offer her heartfelt thanks. Until then, every encounter we had shared had been for Steven and about Steven. In that moment, though, I made an unconscious shift; all contact thereafter would be in support of this woman who had lost her great love.

Supporting Meredith taught me firsthand about grieving, just as helping Steven had taught me important lessons about dying. Once again, I brought "all of me" to this work: no borders, no boundaries, but always trying to lead with service. At different times, I was hospice doctor, grief counselor, and confidante; ultimately I became simply a good friend.

When the idea of the hospice fast inevitably resurfaced, both of us recognized the potential synergy of the two of us teaching together. As partners, we could bring the ceremony of a symbolic death and rebirth to medical people, especially those doing hospice work; and we could help wilderness guides rediscover how rites of passage have always been a dying practice. After months of brainstorming and a few tentative attempts at co-teaching, the potential of the work quickly turned into reality. In the first year of the partnership, we traveled to the desert lands of Eastern California and over to the Big Island of Hawaii. In the second year, we co-led programs in South Africa, Austria, Germany, and Switzerland and back home in the California desert. Along the way, we gave this new curriculum a name: "The Practice of Living and Dying."*

In early 2003, just before my first visit with Steven and Meredith, I began saying to myself and to my closest friends, "My days at the HIV Clinic are numbered."

After fourteen years of service, I still felt deeply connected to many of my patients, and I was thrilled to see them benefiting from the vast improvements in HIV medicine. And yet the job had become confining, at times even boring. In the early years of the epidemic, I had been asked to participate in so many difficult, yet vibrant conversations, and I had been privileged to witness the living out of so many poignant stories. In this new era, however, my job demanded that I focus mostly on biomedical details, forever trying to outwit a frequently mutating virus. When I looked at a list of patients at the start of a clinic, I saw more of an obligation to review labs and to ask about side-effects than an opportunity to deepen human connections. In this version of a rapidly changing job, only "part of me" was needed.

In contrast, "all of me" was often required when I was at someone's deathbed or, later on, when I was in the desert co-leading a course. The more I worked with the dying—on either side of the bridge between literal death and symbolic death—the more it became clear that my time at the HIV Clinic would

---

* See page 175-6 for more information about the Practice of Living and Dying.

soon be over. And yet there was tremendous security in that old, familiar job. Not only did it pay well and offer premium benefits, but my professional identity was deeply attached to this work. "AIDS physician" had long been my primary way of being named in the world. To walk away from the clinic, that part of me would first have to die.

"Yes, my days are numbered," I would quickly add to my friends, "but that number is still in the 1000s."

Looking back, I have to laugh. Having openly given a terminal prognosis to my identity as an AIDS physician, I was still determined to prolong its life for as long as possible. But after my first desert fast over the new millennium, and after crossing the Golden Gate Bridge and bringing "all of me" to Steven's deathbed, that denial was not sustainable. In September of 2005, just short of 1000 days after the idea had first come to me, I quit my job at the HIV Clinic.

The Monday evening following my last week at this job, I threw my own goodbye party. I invited the clinic staff and all of my patients and, for the fifty-plus people who came, I cooked a five-course meal. After we had finished eating, a few friends and patients offered their reflections about my years at the clinic. Then it was my turn to speak.

"Today, Scott 'the AIDS physician' is dying. He's dying so that he can be reborn again into new kinds of work. Let me tell you something about what it is he will be doing . . ."

I switched back into a first-person voice, briefly describing my plan to focus on hospice work and wilderness work.

"One of the things I've already learned from doing end-of-life work is the importance of completing relationships before you die." I introduced the five-part hospice wisdom and then offered an expanded version of "Please forgive me, I forgive you, thank you, I love you, and goodbye," making it as relevant as possible to my time at the clinic.

A magical, unexpected moment came just after I had said the "I love you" part. Turning to the far right and scanning slowly across to the left, I looked at each person, one at a time. By locking my gaze with each set of eyes, I confirmed, again and again, that the "I love you" was true.

I closed the evening by saying to the entire group, "Time now for a final goodbye. But a goodbye only from Scott 'the AIDS physician.' By the end of today, that part of me will be dead, while the rest of me lives on."

So now I am a physician who specializes in supporting life transitions. I am a hospice doctor who sits with the dying in their homes, and I am a rite-of-passage guide who sits with "the dying" out in the desert. This week it's the latter work that I am doing. I am keeping vigil for a group of eleven people who have come to Meredith and me, trusting that together we will hold them well as they look to renew their lifestories.

There is Dianne, a hospice nurse who came to us fifteen months ago in Death Valley, the first time we offered the Ballcourt fast. Never having camped in her life, never having looked inside herself in quite this way, she had been drawn by an inner calling that she couldn't quite name and certainly couldn't explain. During her first solo fast, she discovered that—-despite her good work of helping others to complete their lives—she hadn't been keeping her own life current. She returned home to a year of difficult conversations, many by letter, some in person, and the majority alone with herself. She now rejoins us so she can mark and claim all the work that she has done. Her stated intention: "I am a woman in transition. May I be present in my life and may I continue to show up."

There is Franz, a tai chi teacher who has given the last twenty years of his life to creating a successful institute in Vienna, only to become trapped by the constant demands of running the large organization. He has come to this desert mountain already having had the many difficult conversations that will allow him to step away from this burdensome role. His intention: "I am two twins: a man who has already had enough success in the world and a boy who is full of curiosity. That man is now free to take back the hand of the boy. Together they will love this magnificent life."

There is my longtime friend Sue, a physician with an uncommon compassion for people who are suffering—especially those who are difficult to love, those who are isolated, or those whom others have forgotten. Here on her third extended fast in six years, she has been learning how to offer that same uncommon compassion to herself, and now she has come to mark and to celebrate the work she has done. Her intention: "I am a woman facing east. With the tail wind of Spirit behind me, I am a woman healing."

Along with these three, there are eight other wonderful people. Each one has a story full of pain, triumph, and possibilities. Each one has a desire for transformation. And each one has an intention carefully honed during the months leading up to this ceremony.

When these eleven people return to base-camp, they will need time to begin re-entering their physical bodies and the physical world. Our only significant task that first day back will be relocating as a group to a campground closer to town. There they will have time to eat, to bathe, to socialize, or to do whatever else that is self-nurturing.

The next phase of the return will be the two days of storytelling. Each person, one at a time, will try to describe what happened during the four-day fast, though these words will be just the first version of an evolving story. Meredith and I will receive this first telling, hold it gently, and then take turns offering the story back. The goal of our retelling will be to name the challenges faced, the essential qualities tapped, and the insights gained. We want to help each person see that what happened in the desert was real and true, and we want to support them as they prepare to step back into the bodies of their lives back home.

The work that I am about to do with these people who have symbolically died is much the same as the work that I'm doing at home with people who are literally dying. To both, I offer an open heart, a listening ear, and an engaged imagination—all in service to lifestories that are still unfolding. This work, like my visits with Steven, asks that I bring "all of me." What a great blessing it is to have found work of this kind. Or rather, what a blessing it is that the work has found me.

Scott Eberle
Inyo Mountains, California
May 2006

Resources

The following resource list is offered to those who want to investigate end-of-life issues raised in this book. The entries are not meant to be comprehensive; rather each is a point of entry for further exploration.

Advance Directives & Wills

Many varieties of advance directives exist, but most include at least two basic parts: a living will in which you declare whether or not life-sustaining treatment should be used if you are faced with an irreversible and incurable illness; and the designation of a power of attorney for health care, a person who can act as your surrogate decision maker if you are no longer able. Some advance directives also include a section about what to do with your body after death, including the option of organ donation. Separate from advance directives is the matter of creating a regular will that designates how you want your possessions to be distributed.

Partnership for Caring: America's Voice of the Dying
National Office: 1035 30th Street, NW Washington DC 20007
800-989-9455 / www.partnershipforcaring.org

This program of the National Hospice and Palliative Care Organization provides free resources and information to help people make decisions about end-of-life care and services. Topics covered include advance care planning, caregiving, pain, financial issues, hospice and palliative care, grief and loss. In particular, they have advance directives forms specific for every state, which can be downloaded for free.

NHPCO HelpLine: 800-658-8898

This toll-free helpline provides end-of-life information, including free brochures, advance directives, and contact information for hospices and other end-of-life organizations.

Five Wishes

1-888-5-WISHES (594-7437) / www.agingwithdignity.org

This popular version of a living will allows people to express their "five wishes:" which person you want to make your health care decisions if you are unable; the kinds of medical treatments you want or don't want; how physically comfortable you want to be; how you want people to treat you; and what you want your loved ones to know. To purchase copies, contact Aging with Dignity.

Books

Many guidebooks are available for creating advance directives and/or a regular will. The following is only a short list; check your local library to see which books it has to offer.

Benji O. Anosike. How to Plan Your 'Total' Estate with a Will & Living Will, Without the Lawyer's Fees: the American Will Kit, Usable in All 50 States. East Orange, NJ: Do-It-Yourself Legal Publishers, 2005.

Joy S. Chambers. The Easy Will and Living Will Kit (+ CD-ROM). Naperville, Ill: Sphinx Pub, 2005.

Edward A. Haman. How to Write Your Own Living Will. Naperville, Ill: Sphinx Pub, 2004.

Ethical Wills

An ethical will is a non-legal document that records your memories, stories, beliefs, rituals, values, and/or prayers—the spiritual legacy for which you want to be remembered. The tradition of bequeathing a spiritual legacy is particularly strong in the Jewish culture, having been first described in the Hebrew Bible 3000 years ago. Initially, these ethical wills were transmitted orally, only later to become written documents. In recent years, interest in this practice has grown among people of various religions and cultures.

An ethical will can be addressed to one person or to a larger group of family and/or friends. Once written, the document can be given away immediately, attached to your regular will, and/or read at a memorial service. Some people begin writing an ethical will when they know they are dying, but some do this much earlier in life. It might be written to a newborn, with new entries made at each birthday. It might be something that a couple does together as a way of knowing each other better. Or it might even be written to someone who has already died as a way of keeping that connection alive.

If you want to compose an ethical will, you might include any of the following elements: an opening that addresses to whom you are writing; a description of your family and the events that shaped its history; your own personal story focusing on influential people, places, and events; a recollection of what you most appreciated in life or that which you most regretted; an offering of, or asking for, forgiveness; a description of your values, beliefs, and ideals, including what you wish you had known at an earlier age; a review of rituals and teachings that have been important to you; requests you have for what you would like family or friends to do after you die; and an ending that declares your closing wish or prayer.

BOOKS

Barry K. Baines. Ethical Wills: Putting Your Values on Paper. Cambridge, MA: Perseus Books, 2002.

Rachael Freed. Women's Lives, Women's Legacies: Passing Your Beliefs & Blessings to Future Generations: Creating Your Own Spiritual-Ethical Will. Fairview Press, 2003.

Jack Riemer and Nathaniel Stampfer. So That Your Values Live On:

Ethical Wills & How to Prepare Them. Woodstock, VT: Jewish Lights Pub, 1991

SOFTWARE
The Ethical Will Writing Guide. Visit www.ethicalwill.com for information about software that can guide you through the writing of an ethical will. Baines's book (see above) is also available through this website.

Forgiveness

For many, one the hardest tasks of dying is completing relationships and one of the hardest parts of living is keeping relationships current. At the core of this struggle is the difficult work of forgiveness, both the giving and receiving of it. Any book (including the one you are now holding) will be limited in what it can teach about this highly personal task. The following books are offered merely as possible guideposts during a lifetime of learning.

See also the "Practice of Living and Dying" curriculum, described at the end of this section, for information about an experiential course on forgiveness.

BOOKS
Johann Christoph Arnold. Seventy Times Seven: The Power of Forgiveness. Farmington, PA: The Plough Publishing House, 1997.

Robert Enright. Forgiveness is a Choice: A Step-by-Step Process for Resolving Anger and Restoring Hope. Washington, DC: American Psychological Association, 2001.

Robert D. Enright and Joanna North (editors). Exploring Forgiveness. Madison, WI: The University of Wisconsin Press, 1998.

Pumla Gobodo-Madikizela. A Human Being Died That Night: A South African Woman Confronts the Legacy of Apartheid. Boston: Mariner Books, 2003.

Janis Abrahms Spring. <u>How Can I Forgive You? The Courage to Forgive, the Freedom Not To.</u> New York: Harper Collins Publishers, 2004.

Everett Worthington. <u>Five Steps to Forgiveness: The Art and Science of Forgiving.</u> New York: Crown Publishers, 2001.

Funerals

Over the past few decades, more and more people have been exploring how to be active in the care of the physical body after death and the rituals associated with that. The following are just a few resources about this topic. Visit a nearby library to look for additional references.

FUNERAL CONSUMERS ALLIANCE
33 Patchen Road, South Burlington, VT 05403
800-765-0107 / www.funerals.org

This organization is dedicated to protecting the right of consumers to choose a meaningful, dignified, affordable funeral. At their website is a comprehensive list of non-profit funeral consumer groups throughout the United States.

BOOKS
Carlson, Lisa. <u>Caring for the Dead: Your Final Act of Love.</u> Hinesburg, VT: Upper Access, 1998.

Cochrane, Don S. <u>Simply Essential Funeral Planning Kit.</u> Bellingham, WA and North Vancouver, Canada: Self-Counsel Press, 2002.

Hospice Volunteering

In the early years of the American hospice movement, individual hospices were often staffed by a variable mix of volunteers: whichever people showed up to do the work. Three decades later, the roles that are played on a hospice team are much more defined and include nurses, social workers, chaplains, home health aides, and doctors. Nonetheless, the role of the volunteer continues, having been supported by Medicare regulations.

If you are interested in volunteering at a hospice program, check a local phonebook for a hospice in your area, or contact the NHPCO HelpLine: 800-658-8898. Typically volunteers receive training that will prepare them either for sitting with a person who is dying or supporting someone who is grieving a major loss.

Memorial Services/Rituals

Ritual and ceremony are important parts of marking life transitions, including when someone is dying or after a death. The following is a short list of books that can assist you in creating rituals appropriate to a given situation.

BOOKS
Anderson, Megory. Sacred Dying: Creating Rituals for Embracing the End of Life. Roseville, CA: Prima Publishing, 2001.

Biziou, Barbara. The Joy of Ritual: Spiritual Recipes to Celebrate Milestones, Ease Transitions, and Make Every Day Sacred. New York: Golden Books, 1999.

Feinstein, David, and Mayo, Peg Elliot. Rituals for Living and Dying. San Francisco: HarperCollins: 1990.

Some, Malidoma Patrice. Ritual: Power, Healing and Community. Portland, OR: Swan/Raven, 1993.

Memory Boxes

Memory boxes are a way of collecting important memorabilia so that people and stories won't be forgotten. A box might contain photos, home videos, letters, or other mementos. As memories continue to arise, additional objects can be placed in the box.

Memory boxes have been used by a wide array of people, including bereaved parents who have lost an infant due to miscarriage or early death and elderly people with advancing dementia who are having a difficult time remembering who they are. One of the most poignant examples comes from Africa where so many young children have been orphaned by AIDS or other tragedies. There a memory box is used to hold onto the mementos and stories of a dying or dead parent, so that a child will still receive a legacy from that parent.

The following are guidebooks for making a special memory box, but obviously any box deemed suitable can be used for this purpose.

BOOKS

Anna Corba. <u>Making Memory Boxes: 35 Beautiful Projects.</u> New York: Sterling Publishing Company, 2005.

Barbara Mauriello. <u>Making Memory Boxes: Box Projects to Make, Give, and Keep.</u> Gloucester, Mass: Rockport Publishers, Inc., 2000.

Wilderness Work

The Practice of Living and Dying: The author, in partnership with Meredith Little, offers "The Practice of Living and Dying" curriculum, a bridge between the work of hospice and the practice of wilderness rites. These programs have been held in the deserts of eastern California, across the United States and Europe, and in South Africa.

The author is also available for speaking about hospice care, the difficult conversation in medicine, the universal psychospiritual stages of dying, and the book's main topic, "learning to die in order to live."

SELECTED COURSES IN
THE PRACTICE OF LIVING AND DYING

Dying as a Rite of Passage: This outdoor program of six to nine days is a comprehensive introduction to the Practice of Living and Dying. It is offered to all caregivers—though "caregiver" is defined loosely, understanding that each of us, regardless of profession, is a caregiver to self and to others.

In the Death Lodge: Forgiveness and Reconciliation: This program, also held in a natural setting and six to nine days long, focuses on the work of the Death Lodge, with special attention to the giving and receiving of forgiveness.

The Great Ballcourt Initiation Fast: This advanced program is nearly two weeks in length and features a four-day solo fast in the wilderness. Participants are required to have completed another Practice of Living and Dying course or to have done a three- or four-day wilderness fast.

Other Advanced Training: Additional training is available for people who want to incorporate elements of the Practice of Living and Dying into their own wilderness work or hospice work.

The Practice of Living and Dying courses are part of an array of wilderness programs offered by the School of Lost Borders. Visit the School website for a current schedule of all programs, including the Living and Dying courses.

The School of Lost Borders
P.O. Box 55, Big Pine, CA 93513 / 760-938-3333
www.schooloflostborders.com

Notes

Title Page

[1] Philippe Aries. *The Hour of Our Death.* New York: Alfred A. Knopf, 1981: 300.

Historical Note

[1] Joseph Campbell with Bill Moyers. *The Power of Myth.* New York: Doubleday, 1988: 108.
[2] Steven Foster. *Bound for the Crags of Ithaka: A Romance for Men Going Home.* Big Pine, CA: Lost Borders Press, 2003: 69.

Prologue

[1] Steven Foster. *Under the Skirt of the Dark Goddess.* Unpublished autobiography.

Decision Road

[1] Steven Foster and Meredith Little. *The Roaring of the Sacred River: The Wilderness Quest for Vision and Self-Healing.* Big Pine, CA: Lost Borders Press, 1989, 1997: 31.
[2] Campbell with Moyers. *The Power of Myth*, p. 31.
[3] Arnold van Gennup, translation by Monika Vizedom and Gabrielle Caffee. *The Rites of Passage,* 1907. Chicago: The University of Chicago Press, 1960.
[4] Joseph Campbell. *The Hero with a Thousand Faces.* Princeton: Princeton University Press, 1949: 30.
[5] van Gennup. *The Rites of Passage*, p. 189.
[6] The first known printed accounts of a Land of the Dead are on baked clay tablets from ancient Sumeria in the Tigris-Euphrates Valley north of the Persian Gulf (Alice K. Turner. *The History of Hell.* New York:

Harcourt Brace & Company; 1993: 5).

[7] Howard Rollin Patch. *The Other World: According to Descriptions in Medieval Literature.* Cambridge: Harvard University Press, 1950.

[8] Popol Vuh was first written down anonymously in Quiché Maya utilizing Latin script, some thirty years after the conquering Spaniards had burned all local books. Discovered over a century later, it was translated into Spanish by a priest, a copy of which later resurfaced in 1857 when it was published in Vienna. Multiple translations exist, but Ralph Nelson's is used here (*Popol Vuh: the Great Mythological Book of the Ancient Maya.* Translated by Ralph Nelson. Boston: Houghton Mifflin, 1974).

[9] Nelson. *Popol Vuh,* p. 75.

[10] Ibid.

[11] As just one example, a 1961 study by Donald Oken found that 88% of physicians in a Chicago hospital had the usual practice of not telling cancer patients a true diagnosis, with 56% saying they never or very rarely made an exception to this policy. Despite the high rate of withholding the truth for others, fully 60% of the doctors said they would want to be told by another doctor if they had cancer. Despite the deception with patients, their motives were certainly honorable enough. Many spoke of how a diagnosis of cancer would "deprive a patient of hope" (in 1961, a cancer diagnosis was far more likely to be terminal than it is now). More than three-fourths of these doctors identified the primary determinant of this practice of secrecy as "clinical experience." Data from the survey, however, found no relationship between a desire to conceal or reveal, and a physician's years of experience or age. More to the point, these physicians were functioning at a time when the cultural deception about dying was so deep and pervasive that no other way to practice seemed possible (Donald Oken. What to tell cancer patients: A study of medical attitudes. *JAMA* 1961; 175: 1120-1128).

[12] The modern era of CPR began in 1960 with a report by Kouwenhoven and colleagues that found a 70% survival-to-discharge rate in patients undergoing closed-chest resuscitation (Kouwenhoven WB, Jude JR, Knickerbocker GG. Closed-chest cardiac massage. *JAMA* 1960; 173: 1064-7). In 1993, Schneider and colleagues did a 30-year review of the literature and found that the success rate for CPR had not changed

significantly over those three decades, consistently remaining around 15%. Over that same timeframe, however, they reported a steady decline in the optimism about the value of the procedure (Schneider AP, Nelson DJ, Brown DD. In-Hospital Cardiopulmonary Resuscitation: A 30-Year Review. *JABFP* 1993; 6(2): 91-101).

[13] Steven Foster. *We Who Have Gone Before: Memory and an Old Wilderness Midwife.* Big Pine, CA: Lost Borders Press, 2002: 83.

[14] Foster. *We Who Have Gone Before,* p. 84.

[15] Ibid.

[16] Elisabeth Kübler-Ross. *On Death and Dying: What the dying have to teach doctors, nurses, clergy and their own families.* New York: MacMillan Publishing Co., Inc., 1969.

[17] Campbell. *The Hero with a Thousand Faces.*

[18] Steven Foster. Unpublished diary. 1976.

[19] Black Elk, recorded and edited by Joseph Epes Brown. *The Sacred Pipe: Black Elk's Account of the Seven Rites of the Oglala Sioux.* Norman: University of Oklahoma Press, 1953: 44-66.

[20] Foster. Unpublished diary, 1974.

[21] Foster. Unpublished diary, January 1975.

[22] Meredith Little. Private communication. June 2004.

[23] Virginia Hine. *Last Letter to the Pebble People.* Santa Cruz: Unity Press, 1977.

[24] Hine. *Last Letter to the Pebble People,* p. 55.

[25] Hine. *Last Letter to the Pebble People,* p. ix.

[26] Hine's description of networks can be found in "The Basic Paradigm of a Future Socio-Cultural System" (*World Issues,* April/May 1977). With Luther Gerlach, she also co-authored two books: *People, Power, Change* (Bobbs-Merrill, 1970) and *Lifeway Leap: The Dynamics of Change in America* (University of Minnesota Press, 1972).

[27] Steven Foster with Meredith Little. *The Book of the Vision Quest: Personal Transformation in the Wilderness,* first edition. New York: Island Press, 1980.

[28] Hyemeyohsts Storm. *Seven Arrows.* New York: Harper & Row, 1972.

[29] Little. Private communication, June 2004.

[30] Ibid.

The First Home Visit

[1] Steven Foster. Excerpt from email sent to a friend. January 4, 2003.

[2] Steven Foster. Excerpt from email sent to a friend. January 8, 2003.

[3] Rainer Maria Rilke, translation by David Young. *Duino Elegies,* 1922. New York: W.W. Norton & Company, Inc., 1978: 89-90.

Death Lodge

[1] Steven Foster. *The Great Ballcourt Vision Fast.* Unpublished.

[2] Foster and Little. *The Roaring of the Sacred River,* p. 33.

[3] While the teaching about how to complete a relationship originated from an unknown source, Ira Byock has written a book drawn from that wisdom called, *The Four Things That Matter Most: A Book about Living* (New York: Free Press, 2004). Rather than focusing on just the deathbed completion of a relationship, which necessarily ends with the last step of goodbye, he locates a place in our everyday lives for the first four: offering and receiving forgiveness, gratitude, and love.

[4] Foster. *Under the Skirt of the Dark Goddess.*

[5] Kübler-Ross. *Working It Through.* New York: MacMillan Publishing Co., Inc., 1982: pp. 34-6.

[6] Ibid, p. 34.

[7] Foster. *Under the Skirt of the Dark Goddess.*

[8] Kübler-Ross. *Working It Through,* p. 11.

[9] Kübler-Ross. *Working It Through,* p. 42.

[10] Elisabeth Kübler-Ross. *Death is of Vital Importance: On Life, Death, and Life After Death.* Barrytown, N.Y.: Station Hill Press, 1995: 129.

[11] Kübler-Ross. *Working It Through,* p. 46.

[12] Foster. *Under the Skirt of the Dark Goddess.*

[13] Foster. Unpublished diary, February 19, 1976.

[14] Foster. *Under the Skirt of the Dark Goddess.*

[15] Campbell. *The Hero with a Thousand Faces.*

[16] Foster. *Under the Skirt of the Dark Goddess.*

[17] Ibid.

[18] Ibid.

[19] Ibid.

[20] Foster. Unpublished diary, December 7, 1973.

[21] Foster. Unpublished diary, December 4, 1976.

[22] Foster. *We Who Have Gone Before,* pp. 36-7.

[23] Little. Private communication, January 2004.

[24] Foster. Unpublished diary, December 4, 1976.

[25] Foster. Unpublished diary, September 22, 1975.

[26] Little. Private communication, November 2003.

[27] Little. Private communication, December 2003.

[28] Ibid.

[29] Foster. Unpublished diary, December 30, 1975.

[30] Foster with Little. *The Book of the Vision Quest,* first edition.

[31] Steven Foster with Meredith Little. *The Book of the Vision Quest: Personal Transformation in the Wilderness, revised edition.* New York: Simon & Schuster, 1992: 36.

[32] Little. Private communication, September 2005.

[33] Based on private communication from Meredith Little. September 2005.

[34] Philippe Aries. *The Hour of Our Death.* New York: Alfred A. Knopf, 1981: 300.

[35] Ibid.

The Second Home Visit

[1] Steven Foster. Excerpt from email to the author. January 29, 2003.

[2] Foster. Excerpt from email to the author. March 25, 2003.

[3] Foster. Composite of excerpts from two emails to the author. February 13, 2003 and April 15, 2003.

Purpose Circle

[1] Foster and Little. *The Roaring of the Sacred River,* p. 34.

[2] Steven Foster with Meredith Little. *The Four Shields: The Initiatory Seasons of Human Nature.* Big Pine, CA: Lost Borders Press, 1998: 207.

[3] Erik H. Erikson. *Childhood and Society,* 1950. New York: W.W. Norton & Company, Inc., 1985.

[4] Ibid, p. 269.

[5] William James. *Varieties of Religious Experience: A Study in Human Nature,* 1902. New York: Mentor Edition, 1958: 281.

[6] Campbell. *The Hero with a Thousand Faces.*

[7] Ibid, p. 388.

[8] Campbell explores the theme of becoming "twice-born" in many places. A good introduction can be found in his conversations with Bill Moyers (Campbell with Moyers. *The Power of Myth*).

[9] Campbell. *The Hero with a Thousand Faces,* p. 388.

[10] Guy Claxton. *Hare Brain, Tortoise Mind: Why Intelligence Increases When You Think Less.* Hopewell, NJ: Ecco Press, 1999.

[11] Scott Eberle. Unpublished description of a desert fast. November 2005.

[12] Abraham Maslow. "The Need to Know and the Fear of Knowing." *J Gen Psych* 1963; 68: 119.

[13] Maslow. *Toward a Psychology of Being,* 1968. New York: John Wiley & Sons, Inc., 1999.

[14] Ernest Becker. *The Denial of Death.* New York: The Free Press, 1973: 51-2.

[15] Becker. *The Denial of Death,* p. 66

[16] Becker. *The Denial of Death,* p. 60

[17] Foster. Unpublished diary, December 1980.

[18] David Steindl-Rast. "Learning to Die." Parabola 1977; II (1): 22.

[19] Foster. Unpublished diary, February 1984.

[20] Little. Private communication, August 10, 2003.

[21] Foster. *Bound for the Crags of Ithaka,* p. 32.

The Third Home Visit

[1] Foster. Excerpt from email to the author. April 15, 2003.

[2] Foster. Excerpt from email to the author. April 26, 2003.

The Great Ballcourt

[1] Foster. *The Great Ballcourt Vision Fast.*

[2] Stanislav Grof. *Books of the Dead: Manuals for Living and Dying.* New York: Thames and Hudson; 1994: 24.

[3] In a study published in 1990, Lichter and Hunt documented the dying experience for patients receiving care from Te Omanga hospice in Lower Hutt, New Zealand. For 200 consecutive people dying under

their care, 30% were conscious up to the time of death, 38% became unconscious 0-12 hours before death, 24% were unconscious for 12-24 hours, 7% were unconscious for 24-48 hours, and 1% were unconscious for more than 48 hours (Lichter I, Hunt E. The Last 48 Hours of Life. *J Palliat Care* 1990 Winter; 6(4): 7-15).

[4] In Lichter and Hunt's study (see preceding footnote), 36% of people experienced significant physical symptoms in the last 48 hours of life, including noisy and moist breathing, pain, restlessness, urinary incontinence, shortness of breath, difficulty urinating, nausea and vomiting, sweating, jerking or twitching or plucking, and confusion). Given effective palliative treatment, only 8.5% of them were still visibly suffering at the time of death, with those 17 people experiencing bleeding, respiratory distress, restlessness, pain, heart attack, or regurgitation (Lichter and Hunt. *J Palliat Care* 1990).

In contrast, a 1997 report from Lynn and colleagues looked at deaths for people admitted to a hospital either with a grave illness (mortality rate of 46%) or past the age of 80 (mortality rate of 35%). Of the more than 4,000 people dying, 45% of them were unconscious for three days or more. Of those who were still conscious near the end, 63% of them had difficulty tolerating physical or emotional symptoms in their last three days of life, with pain, shortness of breath, and fatigue being most prevalent. Also 11% of those who died were subjected to a final resuscitation attempt (Lynn J et al. Perceptions by Family Members of the Dying Experience of Older and Seriously Ill Patients. *Ann of Int Med* 1997; 126(2): 97-106).

[5] Maggie Callanan and Patricia Kelley. *Final Gifts: Understanding the Special Awareness, Needs and Communications of the Dying.* New York: Poseidon Press; 1992.

[6] Kenneth Ring. *Life At Death: A Scientific Investigation of the Near-Death Experience.* New York: Quill; 1982.

[7] Michael B. Sabom. *Recollections of Death: A Medical Investigation.* New York: Harper & Row, Publishers; 1982.

[8] Hine. *Last Letter to the Pebble People*, p. 132.

[9] Ibid, p. 133.

[10] Ibid, p. 133.

[11] Ibid, p. 137.

[12] Ibid, p. 138.

[13] Meredith Little. Unpublished diary. January 7, 1976.

[14] Kathleen Singh. *The Grace in Dying: How We Are Transformed Spiritually as We Die.* New York: HarperCollins Publishers; 1998.

[15] Kübler-Ross. *On Death and Dying,* p. 113.

[16] Singh. *The Grace in Dying,* p. 193.

[17] Ibid, pp. 154-160.

[18] M. Scott Peck. *Denial of Soul: Spiritual and Medical Perspectives on Euthanasia and Mortality.* New York: Harmony Books, 1997: 187-88.

[19] Steven Foster. *Bring on the Maggots.* Unpublished.

[20] Ibid.

[21] Ibid.

[22] Steven Foster and Ginnie Hine. Handwritten notes. Unpublished.

[23] Rainer Maria Rilke, translation by M.D. Herter Norton. *The Notebooks of Malte Laurids Brigge,* 1910. New York: W.W. Norton & Company, Inc., 1964: 17.

[24] Foster. Unpublished diary. October 1984.

[25] Foster. *We Who Have Gone Before,* p. 25.

[26] Foster. Excerpt from e-mail sent to a friend. January 8, 2003.

[27] Little. Private communication, August 10, 2003.

[28] Foster. *We Who Have Gone Before,* p. 27.

[29] Hildegard, cited by Matthew Fox and Rupert Sheldrake. *Natural Grace: dialogues on creation, darkness, and the soul in spirituality and science.* New York: Doubleday; 1996: 99.

[30] Callanan and Kelley. *Final Gifts.*

[31] Foster. *We Who Have Gone Before,* p. 218.

The Final Crossing

[1] Steven Foster. Unpublished poem.

Acknowledgments

If it takes a village to raise a child, then it takes almost as many people to create a book. I close, therefore, by remembering and thanking many of the people who have contributed to the making of The Final Crossing.

The writing of this book, and much of what it describes, would never have happened if Steven Foster had not accepted and trusted me so quickly. For the great gift of that trust, and for the friendship that grew out of it, I will be forever grateful. Thank you, Steven.

I would not have written a single sentence of this project without the full support of Meredith Little. Within a week of Steven's death, I went to her with a germ of an idea, asking if she would offer her blessing and if she would read whatever I wrote before it went out into the world. She offered back a resounding "yes" and "yes." Some of the bad early drafts that followed might easily have turned either of these into a "no." Thank you, my dear friend, for continuing to trust in me and in this book, even when there was good reason to have your doubts.

During the first year of writing, early versions of the home visit stories came to me with relative ease, while the "in-between chapters" were much more of a struggle. Deep gratitude to John Hulcoop, Sue Smile, and Patrick Clary for suffering through some of these early drafts, helping me to see what had potential and what needed to be tossed. During the second year, rudimentary versions of the in-between chapters began to take shape, and the overall form of the book became much easier to see. I am grateful to Nancy Jane, Louise Loots, Al Haas, Eric Jamison, and Patti Reiser for confirming and refining that vision. The final sculpting, sanding, and polishing of the book took yet another year, with a multitude of eyes, ears, and hands being essential to this finishing work. For their many contributions, I say a special thank you to Eleanor Haas, Michael Dennis Browne, Robert Kertzner, Sarah Felchlin, Al Mahnken, Anna Baylor, and, yet again, John Hulcoop, Sue Smile, and Nancy Jane.

The importance of Steven's own writings, both published and unpublished, will be obvious to anyone who reads this book. A sincere thanks to Meredith and to Steven's children and stepchildren—Keenan Foster, Christian Foster, Selene Foster, Kevin Smith, and Shelley Miller—for allowing me access to Steven's many volumes of written work and giving permission to have selections reproduced herein. Thank you also to Meredith, Marilyn Foster, Nancy McGraw, and Keenan Foster for entertaining questions about Steven's earlier life and helping me to fill in some important gaps.

The physical shaping of the finished product was the result of many hours of work done by Sarah Felchlin. Thank you, Sarah, for your commitment and your diligence. Gratitude also to Selene Foster and Bill Rhoads for offering their artistic eyes to the creation and completion of the bookcover and to the people at Versa Press for the actual printing of the book.

Though the task of taking this book out into the world has only just begun, several people have already been hugely helpful in planning that process, including Steve Miksis, Andrea Hine, Cherie Plattner, Cazeaux Nordstrom, Natalie Peck, and again Meredith and Bill. Being a "P.R. person" does not come easily to me, so I am grateful for how their ideas and enthusiasm have helped energize this effort.

The process of writing this book was often intertwined with the creation of "The Practice of Living and Dying," the experiential curriculum that Meredith and I have created. The learning and teaching that went into these programs were often inseparable from the learning and teaching that went into this book. Meredith and I offer our thanks to everyone at the School of Lost Borders for your camaraderie and support in the growing of this curriculum, especially Angelo Lazenka, Emerald North, Gigi Coyle, Win Phelps, and Betsy Perluss. Deep appreciation also goes out to the people who have been instrumental in setting up programs around the world: in Hawaii, Tom Sherman and Fran Woollard; in North Carolina, Patti Reiser and Joe Woolley; in Europe, Haiko Nitschke, Franz Redl, Claudia Pichl, Susann Belz, Cornelia Pitsch, Baerbel Kreidt, Edith Oepen, Holger Heiten, Gesa Heiten, Helwig Schinko, Regina Koenig, Katarina Graf, Susan Sully, and Chris Wilton; in South Africa, Valerie Morris, Judy Bekker, and the wonderful people at Educo Africa, especially Mthunzi Funa and Marian Goodman. Gratitude also to the many participants who trusted Meredith and me enough to come to these early programs, and to the many assistants and hosts who helped us to ensure the safety of these people and to hold their stories.

The physician work I do has been taught to me by many, many people over these past two decades. I could write pages and pages of thank you's; instead I offer special mention to John Hulcoop, Rick Flinders, Sue Smile, Anna Baylor, Susan Timko, and the circle of beautiful people at Hospice of Petaluma. I'd be remiss if I didn't also remember my most important teachers over these years: the many people who, like Steven, have trusted me enough to allow me to serve as their physician. I also remember and thank the physicians who supported and cared for Steven before that became my great honor and responsibility: Asao Kamei, Bruce Kelley, and Patrick Clary.

And finally, my undying gratitude and my forever love to Bill Rhoads. Ace, this would never have been possible without you.